DEMOCRACY AND RELATIVISM

Reinventing Critical Theory

Series Editors:
Gabriel Rockhill, Associate Professor of Philosophy, Villanova University; Yannik Thiem, Associate Professor of Philosophy, Villanova University; Jennifer Ponce de León, Assistant Professor of English, University of Pennsylvania

The *Reinventing Critical Theory* series publishes cutting edge work that seeks to reinvent critical social theory for the 21st century. It serves as a platform for new research in critical philosophy that examines the political, social, historical, anthropological, psychological, technological, religious, aesthetic and/or economic dynamics shaping the contemporary situation. Books in the series provide alternative accounts and points of view regarding the development of critical social theory, put critical theory in dialogue with other intellectual traditions around the world and/or advance new, radical forms of pluralist critical theory that contest the current hegemonic order.

Titles in the Series

Commercium: Critical Theory from a Cosmopolitan Point of View, Brian Milstein
Resistance and Decolonization, Amílcar Cabral - Translated by Dan Wood
Critical Theories of Crisis in Europe: From Weimar to the Euro, Edited by Poul F. Kjaer and Niklas Olsen
Politics of Divination: Neoliberal Endgame and the Religion of Contingency, Joshua Ramey
Comparative Metaphysics: Ontology After Anthropology, Pierre Charbonnier, Gildas Salmon and Peter Skafish
The Invention of the Visible: The Image in Light of the Arts, Patrick Vauday - Translated by Jared Bly
Metaphors of Invention and Dissension, Rajeshwari S. Vallury
Technology, Modernity and Democracy, Edited by Eduardo Beira and Andrew Feenberg
A Critique of Sovereignty, Daniel Loick - Translated by Amanda DeMarco
Democracy and Relativism: A Debate, Cornelius Castoriadis - Translated by John V. Garner

DEMOCRACY AND RELATIVISM

A Debate

Cornelius Castoriadis

Translated by John V. Garner

ROWMAN &
LITTLEFIELD
———INTERNATIONAL
London • New York

Published by Rowman & Littlefield International, Ltd.
6 Tinworth Street, London SE11 5AL
www.rowmaninternational.com

Rowman & Littlefield International, Ltd. is an affiliate of
Rowman & Littlefield
4501 Forbes Boulevard, Suite 200, Lanham, Maryland 20706, USA
With additional offices in Boulder, New York, Toronto (Canada), and
London (UK)
www.rowman.com

Copyright © 2020 by Rowman & Littlefield International

All rights reserved. No part of this book may be reproduced in any form
or by any electronic or mechanical means, including information storage
and retrieval systems, without written permission from the publisher,
except by a reviewer who may quote passages in a review.

British Library Cataloguing in Publication Information
A catalogue record for this book is available from the British Library

ISBN: HB 978-1-78661-094-2
ISBN: PB 978-1-78661-095-9
ISBN: Electronic 978-1-78661-096-6

Library of Congress Cataloging-in-Publication Data

Names: Cornelius Castoriadis
Title: Democracy and Relativism: A Debate

CONTENTS

Foreword   vii
    John V. Garner

Note by the Editors of the French Edition   xxxi
    Enrique Escobar, Myrto Gondicas and Pascal Vernay

Introduction   1
    Jean-Louis Prat

Debate with the *MAUSS* Group: 10 December 1994, Paris, France   23
    Cornelius Castoriadis, et al.

References   99

Index   107

FOREWORD

John V. Garner

> The desire and the capacity of citizens to participate in political activities are themselves a political problem and a political task.
> —Cornelius Castoriadis

This book translates the December 1994 meeting between philosopher Cornelius Castoriadis (1922–1997) and the contingent of Francophone intellectuals known as *MAUSS* (extant 1981–present).[1] Castoriadis, born in the Ottoman capital in 1922, had lived in France since 1945 and had developed by the time of this debate a reputation not only for his post-Marxist political 'project of autonomy' but also for his ever-broadening philosophical inquiries into psychology, the sciences and social sciences, and ancient Greek thought, among other areas. *MAUSS* contributors, interested in social theory broadly, had shown some interest in Castoriadis early on.[2] As the text records, this dialogue began with Castoriadis's response to provocative questions sent by Alain Caillé, central figure in *MAUSS*. The text of the dialogue as translated here stems from the debate's complete publication in book format in 2010.[3]

The importance of this encounter for us will quickly become evident to the reader. Its relevance stems not only from the English-speaking world's increasing interest in the work of Castoriadis but also, and above all, from this dialogue's absolutely timely content. Here, I will link the dialogue's themes to three contemporary concerns before commenting, in closing, about matters of context and translation.

RELATIVISM AND DEMOCRACY TODAY

At least three prevalent themes in the Castoriadis-*MAUSS* debate have important contemporary resonances. First, the debate contributes to discussions about the 'post-truth era' through its exploration of the practical consequences of relativism. Second, it speaks to the need to reflect on our institutional-level commitments (e.g. to public spaces, to education, and so on) and on whether and how they enable genuine political engagement and dialogue. Third, it explores important examples of past political engagement, especially the example of Greek democracy, in a way that contextualizes our own era. Emphasis should be placed, in each case, on how the interlocutors model both a respectful form of dialogue and a non-authoritarian approach to intellectual questions.

First, in an age miserably saddled with the epithet 'post-truth era,' the dialogue's opening topic of relativism is timely. We can witness today a multitude of practical consequences relating to the notion that one selects at will one's own facts (e.g. contagions of deceptive memes, widespread distrust in the sciences, the return of collectively eradicated diseases, and so on). Castoriadis certainly recognizes what many relativists do, namely the uniqueness of each person and culture, the dangers in applying local norms transculturally, and the need to avoid trusting blindly in authority or taking one's own cultural norms to be necessary and inalterable.[4] But in this dialogue and elsewhere he establishes a firm, non-relativist support for political programs that would help fulfil the universal promise of an autonomous society with autonomous individuals. This would be, in part, a society in which all people are positively empowered to question themselves and their laws; to deliberate effectively with others about the common good; and, as a collectivity, to establish effective institutions, e.g. ones that make possible their continuation in such practices.[5] Such a 'project of autonomy' would even enable people to relativize these very commitments. Is this an impossible space for Castoriadis to occupy? This question had perplexed Alain Caillé, Serge Latouche, and others for a long time.[6]

For Castoriadis, one must begin by recognizing the historical fragility not only of autonomy and democracy but also of the very possibility of 'relativizing' one's own understanding, perhaps defined as comparing oneself and one's culture with others in such a way that one sees those other practices as possible and as possibly better in significant ways. This task of making the familiar strange, or of 'breaking the closure' of traditional thought (as Castoriadis calls it), is an important part, among many others, of the project of autonomy.[7] Yet relativizing in this sense is not the same thing as a relativism that would pretend all cultures are equally preferable. Such a relativism relies for its possibility on the historically contingent possibility-to-relativize in general. Now, when one relativizes in general, one performs, or practically activates, a preference for the possibility-to-relativize, an option not presently available to all. In doing so, one of course fails to activate many other cultural possibilities and also excludes those practices that presently oppose it. Yet, unlike the mere relativizer, the relativist goes further. Since relativism's possibility depends on the possibility-to-relativize generally, whenever the relativist claims that no culture is especially preferable, he or she in fact enacts a special preference for the historical possibility-to-relativize while ignoring or denying that preference at the same time.

Hence, Castoriadis might be said to relativize relativism. But this move must be understood not as a dismissal of it but rather as a kind of protection of its underlying possibility. If relativism treats its own historical possibility as an *exception* to its rule of 'equal preferability,' then Castoriadis instead promotes a universal *inception* of the broader possibility-to-relativize. That is, he affirms it as one distinct historical possibility, situates it among other possibilities (many of which are presently opposed to it), and defends its activation as one among many preferable parts of the larger project of autonomy that it helps enable. And by affirming that all should be enabled to potentially practice it, Castoriadis thereby commits himself to promoting it to others as an option and fighting against those cultural practices that would presently try to destroy it.[8]

This move – critical but protective of relativism's underlying possibility – leads directly to Castoriadis's subsequent metaphysical and political points. First, Castoriadis is appropriately asked to clarify how he differs from Claude Lefort. After all, he had spent the early part of his career working with him (in *Socialisme ou Barbarie* and elsewhere); both struggled for decades against totalitarianism; both heralded versions of democracy; and Lefort had debated *MAUSS* on an earlier occasion, with Castoriadis reportedly present.[9] Lefort, however, proposed a modern democracy that makes political power – held by the royalty in the old regime – into an 'empty' space of conflict where no view is principally affirmed, i.e. a space of 'indeterminacy.'[10] Castoriadis, by contrast, appears to see Lefort's position as pretending to affirm a political space of possibility that does not affirm any possibility, even itself.[11] Castoriadis, by contrast, argues that at the heart of democracy – precisely because it lies at the heart of being itself – is not indecision, nor an indefinite emptiness, but rather a positive creativity, i.e. a power-to-institute-something-definite, a power to 'create determinations.'[12]

Hence, when he promotes democracy, Castoriadis does not leave political possibilities indeterminate but rather affirms the positive exigency to enable each person to occupy the space of public self-determination, i.e. the creative, instituting social power itself.[13] Castoriadis thus speaks of true politics (*la politique*) as the assuming of responsibility for this original creation, and contrasts it with the typical political activity (*le politique*) of channelling, managing, organizing, or even resisting already-instituted powers (e.g. state power, capitalist power, prejudices of the populace, and so on). True politics occurs when one shares publically in creating definite, positive projects (thus questioning extant ones); inventing laws and self-limitations (thus questioning old ones); and establishing institutional arrangements that help each and all to assume that very practice. But since this possibility – i.e. of the public space – is historically fragile and rare, it follows that making institutional supports that nourish political engagement is required. We must invent or sustain the means encouraging political participation by all, even ones as simple as authentically open meeting places, libraries, schools, and so on.

At this point, Castoriadis – and we too – must recognize many features of contemporary life that hinder participation in the instituting public power. These include traditional forms of political or cultural life that disallow or discourage public participation in legislating (or the questioning of extant legislation); contemporary modes of privatization and capitalistic domination (i.e. the manipulation of desires and public spaces as part of profiteering); failures to establish positive educational opportunities that facilitate collective participation (i.e. lack of *paideia* or 'education in autonomy'); and so on.[14] At the individual level, blocks also appear due to widespread lack of interest, economic hardship, distraction by technological devices, psychological disorders, and so on, all of which are obviously problems, occurring as they do on a mass scale, linked at least partly with larger failures of politics. Thus, what is important about the social critique offered in this debate is that it is not motivated – neither in Castoriadis's case nor in the case of *MAUSS* – by a simple oppositional mindset, nor by a preference for the new or old for their own sake. It is motivated, on the one hand (*MAUSS*), by an understanding of the importance of basic human sociality and, on the other hand (Castoriadis), by a positive commitment to political participation, especially the lucid, overt, and dialogical asking of the question 'What are the ends of human life?'[15]

Second, an additional contemporary challenge is presaged in this debate. For, correlative to the dishonest form of relativism mentioned above is a dishonest and destructive pseudo-individualism. Self-proclaimed 'individuals' each express their individualism by all using the same devices, all absorbing the same news sources, all sharing the same memes, or the like.[16] Amidst this confused and false individualism a sort of absorption in imagined communities is correlated. In some camps, the massively privileged proclaim themselves members of oppressed victim-groups; in other camps, the slightest offence to a social norm immediately provokes a contagious flare-up of condemnations from those collectively more 'in the know'; elsewhere, students unite in support for the 'right' of a prejudicial speaker ('It's free speech!') until protestors arrive ('You're opposing free speech!'); and so on.[17] Such inversions or perversions of emancipatory strategies, of solidarity, and so on have opened the door for, among other things, hack-intellectuals, emboldened by YouTube popularity, to sell base prejudice in the guise of 'evolutionary psychology'; plain arrogance in the guise of 'recovering masculinity'; or social heteronomy and authoritarian politics in the guise of retrieving the 'wisdom' of our ancestors.

In this sad climate, good examples of at least two practices are both needed and possible for us. On the one hand, we need examples of what we might call *interlocutory individuals*, i.e. people in process of achieving an individuality and character via engagements with others who challenge them, especially through intellectual engagements genuinely calling their own practical principles and identity into question.[18] Available to us, if we try, are opportunities for an individuality achieved not by materialist consumerism, nor by immersion in identity-group echo-chamber politics, nor by the 'nihilism' of merely being-against-things, but instead by way of a genuine commitment to learning.[19] The widespread phenomenon of 'fact denial' today cannot be challenged by blasting people with facts; one must first of all care to institute oneself as a learner. And such self-institution *can* be encouraged, enabled, and supported. Learning leans on dialogue, which, in turn, leans on primary sociality (Caillé) as well as public spaces, research spaces, spaces for relativization, and so on (Castoriadis). We can ignore all of this and continue to be socially formed anyway, or we can positively form ourselves by establishing supports that help us become certain kinds of people, i.e. those who value learning over self-closure and new friends over new cars. Happily, this debate itself offers us some hope for the future of genuine dialogue.[20]

On the other hand, we likewise need examples of responsible *scholarship*, especially regarding the inherently fragile remnants of past human intellectual engagements. In a time when our academy is heavily armed with much-justified criticisms of the traditional 'Western canon,' how might an old debate among privileged

Westerners about the value of 'the West' contribute to the promotion of global thinking, East and West, North and South? Without expanding heavily on the following points, I would just mention three heuristic principles we might draw from this debate on this theme. First, certainly, we must fight for increased, intensive scholarship on under-recognized and global contributions to effective thinking and effective autonomy.[21] Second, we must work against authoritarian co-options of intellectual remnants – e.g. texts, art, monuments, and social significations broadly – regardless of whether they have been traditionally included or excluded from any canon. Third, regarding the intellectual remnants that have already been disfigured to fit into the heteronomy propaganda machines, we must show that the lessons harboured in them actually obliterate, with their own arguments, any such authoritarian appeals, when they (frequently) do so.

If these last two paragraphs together ring true, then perhaps we may benefit from rethinking the sorts of cultural background commitments that foster autonomy and dialogue.[22] The debate's third point of relevance for us today thus consists in its engagement with historical democracy, specifically the Greek example.[23] If, in the postcolonial context, Caillé is particularly concerned to combat ethnocentrism, then Castoriadis argues that the Greeks of the fifth century B.C.E. can assist us in just this struggle. The aspects of autonomy partly emergent there serve to undermine ethnocentrism, heteronomy broadly, and *a fortiori* any mindset that would embrace Greek culture as a kind of authority. Past instances of autonomy offer us not models but only 'germs' (seeds) for further development.[24] Thus, contrary to any supposed superiority of things Greek, to any supposed special holistic harmony of Athenian society (Schiller, etc.), or to any supposed pre-Platonic closeness with Being (Heidegger, etc.), Castoriadis highlights the fragility of the limited creation of autonomy there, which was itself emergent within an often troubling larger culture.[25] Nonetheless, some Greeks did partly achieve a lucidity regarding the contingency of their own and others' institutions; they glimpsed the ongoing nature of human self-creativity, individual and collective. This realization showed, in turn, that societies and individuals need to create and recreate the conditions that make it possible to recognize this self-creation and to ask what one is to do with it. What should our constitution say? What, after all, is good or just? If we expect such questioning to impact the world, then we require not only the institutional supports for carrying out the at-best-temporary solutions we decide on but also – and primarily – the institutional supports for continuing to engage in this very act of self-questioning, deliberation, and so on. Hence, if philosophy is partly emergent in Greece as a commitment to *endlessly rethinking* things, also partly emergent there, correlatively, is the recognition that one must take up the practical activity of *decisively determining* things (i.e. making contingent, revisable decisions, institutions, and laws that are never once-and-for-all).[26] Indeed, the most pressing lessons from ancient democracy are those displaying a positive institutional commitment to establishing each citizen as self-critical and competent to govern.[27] Surely such lessons are as valuable as ever today when our oligarchies proudly wear the mask of democracy.[28] By drawing on these elements, Castoriadis is in effect undermining the very claim that a historical example like Athens should be taken as an authority.[29] Historical examples offer us merely helpful remnants, ones that might assist in a new autonomous natality.[30] We always lean on them (even and especially when we call our inherited institutions into question); but they do not determine us.[31]

At a different level, certainly, one factual matter might have been presented as more open for debate in Castoriadis's argument. Specifically, he makes the empirical claim that before the ancient Greeks there was no effective social project of autonomy. New evidence and arguments might arise on this issue.[32] That said, Castoriadis typically speaks of the Greeks as the first partial institution of 'effective' autonomy.[33] This qualifier implies that one is not only personally self-critical (which is found in many global ancient traditions) but also that a culture builds material supports for autonomous thought and collective action.[34] It *matters* whether we build education systems, public displays for the laws, or, especially, the very spaces (literal or figurative) in which we can assemble and deliberate publically (i.e. now globally) about what should even count as a public matter.[35] 'Effective' autonomy requires that we exercise some such material commitments. Therefore, to truly challenge Castoriadis's empirical claim, one would need to show that earlier societies exhibited such material commitments. For, we do have some such evidence in the Greek case. Beyond Castoriadis's examples, we might think, for instance, of the *kleroterion* machines, i.e. the devices used in democratic Athens for selecting certain officeholders by sortition. Such tools obviously cannot make a society egalitarian, much less autonomous. A *kleroterion* in particular would not even be a necessary condition for democracy. But some such material supports are needed.[36] Hence, if evidence of a meaningful social *and* material commitment to autonomous self-institution arises elsewhere, then evidently the empirical claim must be emended. This would not be to say that effective democracy did not also begin in Greece, since independent creations can multiply instantiate autonomy. But it would disrupt any claim about chronological priority.

Regardless, Castoriadis's key point here is that ethnocentrism is inconsistent with and positively undermined by the project of autonomy. Thus, when asked whether the partial autonomy in some medieval cities resulted from renewed interest in ancient Greek thought, Castoriadis reverses this suggestion and argues that the burgeoning autonomy drove the return to the Greeks.[37] After all, if ever one were to try to establish autonomy because some prior society did so, or because Castoriadis's work supports autonomy, then one would, by definition, take the law of action as dictated from elsewhere. That would be heteronomy. But, by contrast, to say that whenever we institute ourselves anew we must 'lean on' established conditions, seek out additional extant ones, take them up, modify them, and so on – this is precisely what autonomous societies lucidly recognize.

Tragically, mindless, even fascist, appeals to some supposed authority of 'our past' frequently arise; we hear endless calls to follow our ancestors *because* they are 'our ancestors.'[38] That is one reason why there remains a need for, among many other things, conscientious scholarship regarding the intellectual and political past of autonomous social institutions, i.e. scholarship that helps reveal how those very remnants undermine projects that appeal to them as authorities. But this also means that we must reject any simple solutions to the 'Western canon' problem, especially anti-historical proposals. Anti-historical philosophy, for its part, risks merely enabling dominant, heteronomous imaginaries; it denies us the opportunity to relativize our era and thus to recognize, for one, our own destructive form of relativism.

CONTEXT AND TRANSLATION

For more details on the context of this meeting, see the following introduction by Jean-Louis Prat. He reveals surprising links between the interlocutors and clearly depicts the historical backdrop, especially in relation to Marx and the post-1989 context. My additional contributions to grasping the context of the debate are the following four points.

First, each figure in the volume has an individually interesting trajectory. Louis Baslé is an economist and professor at Université de Picardie Jules Verne. Alain Caillé, in addition to cofounding *MAUSS*, is now emeritus professor of sociology at Université de Paris-X. Jacques Dewitte has authored several books on political philosophy and gift-related themes. Anne-Marie Fixot is teacher and wide-ranging researcher at Université de Caen. Serge Latouche, in addition to cofounding *MAUSS*, is emeritus professor of economics at Université de Paris-XI and works largely on degrowth. Chantal Mouffe is professor of political theory at the Centre for the Study of Democracy at the University of Westminster and author of numerous works of political philosophy. Jean-Louis Prat is also a *MAUSS* contributor, by the way, and is the author of *Introduction à Castoriadis* (Paris: La Découverte, 2007).

As for Castoriadis's broader trajectory, we should bear in mind that his thought was always responsive to the exigencies of the present. His earlier writings are marked by a heterodox Marxism and a special emphasis on workers' councils. During the period of *Socialisme ou Barbarie* (1948–1967), however, he eventually broke with Marxism and in the 1970s leaned increasingly on psychoanalytical concepts both theoretically and as a practitioner. The work generally considered his magnum opus, *The Imaginary Institution of Society*, emerged in 1975 (consisting partly of a major writing from 1964 to 1965). After his attainment of an academic position in 1979, he dealt in the 1980s with broader fields including Soviet studies, biology, ecology, Greek philosophy, and mathematics. By 1994, Castoriadis's work had come increasingly to emphasize the widespread decline of popular political engagement in the West. This decline corresponded to the rise of a culture of 'generalized conformism' integral with a 'pseudo-individualism.'[39] Blind trust in technological and scientific development, combined with popular concern only for the guarantee of pleasures, formed a culture of 'insignificance.'[40] These critiques link up with Castoriadis's opposition in this debate to representative democracy, which he sees as promoting deferral of political responsibility to the representative class. The pseudo-justification for such abdication resides in the liberal imaginary of an ideal society as allowing and encouraging (whether inadvertently or by design) an apolitical private life. By contrast, Castoriadis continued to promote the exigency for popular investment in public self-institution (especially investment in the formation of a politically prepared populace). This project, he argued, requires investment in a truly public space (*ekklēsia*), as kept distinct from the private (*oikos*), which in turn supports a mixed space (*agora*) not co-opted by either private interests or the state.[41] In this light, his emphasis on direct democracy, on display here, indicates not only his preference for a kind of regime but also his promotion of a new or renewed culture of active engagement, i.e. a culture both expecting and enabling the participation of everyone in self-institution and self-limitation.

Second, note that section titles and editorial notes were added to the French edition. It should not be assumed that they were approved by Castoriadis since he had already passed. The reader should also keep in mind that this debate occurred orally and in person. I have attempted to capture the spontaneous nature of the language by, for example, retaining incomplete sentences on some occasions, using contractions, and so on. When interlocutors do use technical terms I have generally appealed to existing translations of their work. Finally, bear in mind that quotations and anecdotes emerge on the fly, and thus some are inexact paraphrases (some tellingly so) or are unconfirmed. While the editors have supplied information on many citations, I have also added some notes or expanded upon existing ones, and these are marked '—Trans.' All other notes are translated from the French, with English-language publications substituted for the French ones when they exist in print.

Third, there are several key terms readers should mentally mark. These fall into two categories: technical terms and terms presenting translation inexactitude. When such terms have arisen, footnotes have generally been added. In lieu of a separate glossary, what follows is a list of some of the more important of these terms with the location of the comment. All terms below are Castoriadis's unless otherwise marked:

- *agora*: page 89, note 29.
- anonymous collective: page 88, note 22.
- arrangement (Fr: *disposition*): page 93, note 55.
- creation: pages 87-88, notes 21 and 23.
- effective autonomy: page xvi.
- *ekklēsia*: page 89, note 29.
- ensemblist-identitary: page 20, note 30.
- germ (Fr: *germe*): page 86, note 9.
- the gift: page 84, note 2 (*MAUSS* terminology).
- heteronomy: page xxiv, note 12 and page 21, note 40.
- indeterminacy (Fr: *indétermination*): page 85, note 7 (Lefort terminology).
- instituting imaginary: page 88, note 22.
- magistrate: page 93, note 58.
- *oikos*: page 89, note 29.
- *paideia*: page 92, note 53.
- *phronēsis*: page 97, note 83.
- the political (Fr: *le politique*): page 86, note 12.
- politics (Fr: *la politique*): page 86, note 12.
- primary sociality: page 90, note 33 (*MAUSS* terminology).
- radical imagination: page 88, note 22.
- rational mastery: page 89, note 30.

- secondary sociality: page 90, note 33 (*MAUSS* terminology).

I have not produced a special note for the term 'autonomy' since the challenge of the whole volume is to develop an account of this term. For a set of invaluable essays elucidating Castoriadis's technical terminology more fully, see Suzi Adams, ed., *Cornelius Castoriadis: Key Concepts* (London: Bloomsbury, 2014).

Lastly, readers introducing themselves to Castoriadis's broader thinking might benefit from exploring the following resources. For a broad collection of Castoriadis's essays, see *The Castoriadis Reader*, ed. and trans. David A. Curtis (Oxford: Blackwell, 1997). For wide-ranging intellectual conversations with Castoriadis, see *Postscript on Insignificance: Dialogues with Cornelius Castoriadis*, trans. Gabriel Rockhill and John V. Garner (New York: Continuum, 2011), with a helpful introduction by Gabriel Rockhill. For a basic introduction to Castoriadis, see John V. Garner, 'Cornelius Castoriadis,' *Internet Encyclopedia of Philosophy* (2011/2015), https://www.iep.utm.edu/castoria/. For a more expansive introduction, see Suzi Adams, *Castoriadis's Ontology: Being and Creation* (New York: Fordham University Press, 2011). For a study especially relevant for those with interest in the sciences, see Jeff Klooger, *Castoriadis: Psyche, Society, Autonomy* (Boston: Brill, 2009). Finally, for those who read French, indispensable is the expansive intellectual biography by François Dosse, *Castoriadis: Une vie* (Paris: La Découverte, 2014). For general bibliographical information, see the Agora International Website, http://www.agorainternational.org; the Association Castoriadis website, http://www.castoriadis.org; and the bibliography of Claude Helbling, https://independent.academia.edu/ClaudeHelbling.

In closing, I would like to thank Rowman & Littlefield International for their support in this project; the reviewers for their helpful suggestions; Gabriel Rockhill and the Villanova Translation Workshop for introducing me, ten years ago, to the intrinsic value of translation; and above all my colleagues, friends, and family for their support, especially Charlie Strong for his valuable editorial suggestions. Thanks to Enrique Escobar for the kind offer of assistance and for elucidating several passages. Lastly, thanks above all to my wife Carly for her constant support and my daughter Eve for her helpful naps and playful interruptions.

NOTES

1. The acronym *MAUSS* stands for *Mouvement Anti-Utilitariste en Sciences Sociales* (Anti-Utilitarian Movement in the Social Sciences). On the group's formation and relation to the thought of its namesake, Marcel Mauss, see Prat's 'Introduction,' this volume.

2. See mentions of Castoriadis as early as Alain Caillé, 'Éditorial : La Non-utilité des femmes,' *Bulletin du MAUSS*, no. 10 (1984). According to Caillé, 'For two years Castoriadis pressed me to invite him to come debate with us' (François Dosse, *Castoriadis : Une vie* (Paris: La Découverte, 2014), 219).

3. See Cornelius Castoriadis, *Démocratie et relativisme. Débat avec le MAUSS* (Paris: Mille et Une Nuits, 2010). Portions of the debate had been published in the group's journal *La Revue du MAUSS semestrielle*, nos. 13 and 14 (1999).

4. Compare to Serge Latouche: 'The universality of transhistorical and ontological values is an illusion, like Plato's shadows. Our dislike of other people's barbarous customs is not founded on a respect for truly universal values, but for our own Western *reasons* – that is all' (Serge Latouche, *The Westernization of the World: Significance, Scope and Limits of the Drive Towards Global Uniformity* (Cambridge: Polity Press, 1996), 125; passage noted in Dosse, *Castoriadis*, 439).

5. On all these points, see, for example, Cornelius Castoriadis, 'Done and To Be Done,' in *The Castoriadis Reader*, ed. and trans. David A. Curtis (Oxford: Blackwell, 1997), 361–417; and Castoriadis, Cornelius,

'Power, Politics, Autonomy,' in *Philosophy, Politics, Autonomy: Essays in Political Philosophy*, ed. and trans. David. A. Curtis (New York: Oxford University Press, 1991), 143–74.

6. In 1987 Caillé had already written, with a light, critical irony: 'Certainly, all imaginaries are equal, as Castoriadis writes, since all of them are equally arbitrary inasmuch as they are really "radical." But, he adds, there is one of them that is nevertheless more equal than the others, i.e. ours, the only one that knows, itself, how to think itself' (Alain Caillé, 'Présentation : Développement, éthique et politique,' *Bulletin du MAUSS*, no. 24 (December 1987), 3). See also Dosse, *Castoriadis*, 219, 317.

7. See Cornelius Castoriadis, 'Breaking the Closure: Cornelius Castoriadis in Dialogue with Robert Legros,' in *Postscript on Insignificance: Dialogues with Cornelius Castoriadis*, trans. Gabriel Rockhill and John V. Garner (New York: Continuum, 2011), 93–107.

8. Hence, I read Castoriadis inclusively, as affirming the compatibility of *some* version of autonomy with *some* possible version of the variety of historical cultures. This is despite the fact that most historical cultures most of the time manifest themselves in their heteronomous versions, incompatible with autonomy. On this topic, see also Cornelius Castoriadis, 'Reflections on Racism,' in *World in Fragments: Writings on Politics, Society, Psychoanalysis, and the Imagination*, ed. and trans. David A. Curtis (Stanford: Stanford University Press, 1997), 19–31.

9. The themes of the Lefort debate are represented in Claude Lefort, 'Réflexions sur le projet du MAUSS,' *La Revue du MAUSS semestrielle*, no. 2 (1993), 61–79. See also Dosse, *Castoriadis*, 219. On *Socialisme ou Barbarie*, see Prat's 'Introduction,' page xxiv, note 14, this volume. The reader should bear in mind that Castoriadis and Lefort had a major falling out in 1980 from which they never recovered. See Dosse, *Castoriadis*, 237–241.

10. See Claude Lefort, *Democracy and Political Theory*, trans. David Macey (Cambridge: Polity Press, 1988), 17–19.

11. See Dosse, *Castoriadis*, 240: 'Lefort thinks democracy as against power, as a force assigned to no institutional site, as an empty site that

incites one to vigilance, in a posture of resistance against all excess in the exercise of political power. Castoriadis, on the contrary, tries to think a political horizon in which power can be incarnate in an autonomous society accomplishing a genuine democratic practice.' In short, for Castoriadis, 'the exercise of political power and democracy need not be considered as outside of one another [. . .].' Hence, Castoriadis's critique of Lefort appears to parallel his point about relativism. The possibility of resisting power (Lefort) hinges on affirming the positive enabling conditions for resistance, which in turn requires engagement in positive politics (*la politique*), beyond resistance (Castoriadis).

12. Castoriadis argues that genuinely new forms of life can and do emerge (which, in effect, always also take up and modify existing forms). Yet, it is possible – and frequent – for social or individual creativity to be expressed in a self-closing way: they may try merely to reproduce existing conditions, to deny self-creation, or to attribute their self-creation to another source. While heteronomy at the social and individual levels thus ensues, each instance of heteronomy is still a unique creation. Hence every culture creates, but not all of them create or sustain the possibility of reflection on that creativity. See also page 87, note 21 and page 88, note 23, this volume.

13. Castoriadis sometimes refers to the ongoing creation at the social-historical level as the work of the 'anonymous collective.' See page 88, note 22, this volume.

14. Thus, Castoriadis does not affirm that all opinions are equal but rather affirms the *project* of generating, for all, the possibility of equal meeting. This project depends on, among other things, effective education: 'The equal effective possibility of participation requires that everyone has effectively been granted all the conditions for such participation' (Cornelius Castoriadis, 'Democracy as Procedure and Democracy as Regime,' trans. David A. Curtis, in *Constellations* 4, no. 1 (April 1997), 6). See also Ingerid S. Straume, *'Paideia,'* in Adams, ed. *Cornelius*, 143–53.

15. See especially the engagement with Chantal Mouffe in the dialogue.

16. This sentence emulates Castoriadis's comment: 'Even if there were a society, metaphorically speaking, a million times more "individualist" than the current society, this individualism would be a *social* phenomenon. The so-called individuals who indulge themselves in the most total individualism would be as much taken up in the social imaginary as whomever else [. . .]. What we call individualism consists in that, at eight thirty, in millions of French homes, everyone turns the same knob in order to watch the same show. There you have it, individualism.' See Cornelius Castoriadis, 'Contribution de Cornelius Castoriadis (philosophe, EHESS),' *Politix* 1, no. 1 (Winter 1988), 17.

17. Doubtless the widespread phenomenon of collective identities founded on scapegoating and counter-scapegoating suggests that the work of René Girard may prove useful in this analysis. See, for example, René Girard, *Violence and the Sacred*, trans. Patrick Gregory (Baltimore: Johns Hopkins University Press, 1977).

18. Numerous editions of *La Revue du MAUSS* display respectful internal divergences as well as explorations of outside challenges to its own core theses. Castoriadis himself went through extraordinary intellectual upheavals several times (see pages 64-65, this volume).

19. On 'nihilism,' see Simone de Beauvoir, *Ethics of Ambiguity*, trans. Bernard Frechtman (New York: Citadel, 1976), 52–68.

20. Castoriadis's critique of transcendent hope is not inconsistent with hope more broadly and immanently defined. See Cornelius Castoriadis, 'The Greek *Polis* and the Creation of Democracy,' in *Philosophy, Politics, Autonomy: Essays in Political Philosophy*, ed. and trans. David. A. Curtis (New York: Oxford University Press, 1991), 102–3.

21. See especially page 37 this volume, where Castoriadis argues that global cultures stand to 'transform' future instantiations of autonomy in fundamentally helpful ways. Compare to Suzi Adams, 'Castoriadis and Ricoeur on the Hermeneutic Spiral and the Meaning of History: Creation, Interpretation, Critique,' in Suzi Adams, ed., *Castoriadis and Ricoeur in Discussion: On Human Creation, Historical Novelty, and the Social Imaginary* (Lanham, MD: Rowman & Littlefield, 2017), 131, which suggests that Castoriadis's position risks closing down research on

'intercultural versions of autonomy.' While Castoriadis could also be read as opening up such research, he does sometimes use language seemingly dismissive of cultures wholly rather than piecemeal. See Johann P. Arnason, 'Castoriadis and Ricoeur on Meaning and History: Contrasts and Convergences,' in Suzi Adams, ed., *Castoriadis and Ricoeur*, 67. See also notes 25, 29, and 31 just below.

22. Differences aside, an absolute separation between real and fictional dialogue (e.g. of Plato) qua dialogue seems unwarranted. There are fictionalizing aspects, i.e. elements of performance, inexactitude, caricature, and the like even in a living dialogue. And, on the other hand, as for Plato in particular, Gadamer seems right to see the dialogues as attempts to capture the spirit of living discussions. See Hans-Georg Gadamer, 'Plato's Unwritten Dialectic,' in *Dialogue and Dialectic: Eight Hermeneutical Studies of Plato*, trans. P. Christopher Smith (New Haven: Yale University Press, 1980), 126. That said, Castoriadis certainly expressed distrust of the political significance of Plato (and of fourth century B.C.E. Greece broadly) relative to the fifth-century Greek achievement. See, for example, Cornelius Castoriadis, *On Plato's* Statesman, trans. David A. Curtis (Stanford: Stanford University Press, 1999). See also Dosse, *Castoriadis*, 377–79. On a possible entente between Castoriadis and Plato, see Sophie Klimis, 'La Pensée au travail. Réinventer l'autonomie à partir de Platon,' in *Cornelius Castoriadis. Réinventer l'autonomie*, ed. Blaise Bachofen et alii (Paris: Éditions du Sandre, 2008), 235–49. See also John V. Garner, *The Emerging Good in Plato's* Philebus (Evanston: Northwestern University Press, 2017), 29–31, 39–66, and 90–95.

23. For Castoriadis's engagement with the Greek *poleis* (and not just with Athens, as there were many examples), see, for starters, 'Greek *Polis*' as well as his extensive lectures on ancient Greek imaginary: Cornelius Castoriadis, *D'Homère à Héraclite, Ce qui fait la Grèce, tome 1. Séminaires 1982–1983* (Paris: Éditions du Seuil, 2004); *La Cité et les lois, Ce qui fait la Grèce, tome 2. Séminaires 1983–1984* (Paris: Éditions du Seuil, 2008); and *Thucydide, la force et le droit, Ce qui fait la Grèce, tome 3. Séminaires 1984–1985* (Paris: Éditions du Seuil, 2011).

24. On the 'germ' metaphor, see page 86, note 9, this volume. On the global sites of autonomy, see Prat's 'Introduction,' this volume.

25. Castoriadis frequently criticizes ancient Athenian slavery, the status of women, the principle of autochthony, their restriction of autonomous self-institution to the political realm, their limited enabling of individual autonomy, and, among other things, their downfall resulting from failure to engage in the self-limitation required in every democracy. He thus strongly emphasizes the need to transcend their example. See Cornelius Castoriadis, 'The Greek and the Modern Political Imaginary,' in *World*, 84–107; and Castoriadis, 'Power,' 143–74. See also Dosse, *Castoriadis*, 360. Furthermore, Castoriadis expressed near despair regarding modern Greek culture (i.e. what he called its racism and attachment to Greek Orthodoxy); and he harboured a perhaps excessive disdain for Byzantine culture. See Dosse, *Castoriadis*, 351, 354.

26. Castoriadis, 'Power,' 163–64.

27. See Ingerid S. Straume, 'Castoriadis, Education and Democracy,' in Ingerid S. Straume and Giorgio Baruchello, eds., *Creation, Rationality, and Autonomy: Essays on Cornelius Castoriadis* (Copenhagen: NSU Press, 2013), 203–28.

28. Aristotle famously comments that elected leaders correlate to oligarchy, while sortition aligns with democratic equality. See Aristotle, *Politics*, 1294b8. For an excellent discussion of the misuse of the democratic title today, see Gabriel Rockhill, 'What Is the Use of Democracy?: Urgency of an Inappropriate Question,' trans. John V. Garner, in *Counter-History of the Present: Untimely Interrogations into Globalization, Technology, Democracy* (Durham: Duke University Press, 2017), 51–102.

29. Three moments in this dialogue are potentially subject to misinterpretation. First, note that Castoriadis says there is a 'privilege' of Western culture found in its autonomy-aspects (see page 28, this volume). We should read this, however, as praise of autonomy, not of the West; autonomy would constitute the 'privilege' of any culture in which it emerges. Likewise, second, his critique of the 'traditional Indian or Chinese person' (page 34) or the 'believing Jew' (page 65) should be read

with emphasis squarely on the terms 'traditional' and 'believing,' which implies heteronomy in this context. Qua traditional or believing (in the *precise* sense Castoriadis specifies), but *not* qua Chinese, Indian, or Jewish, these cases are treated as failing to instantiate autonomy. But clearly those cultures can, like others, come to instantiate autonomy while remaining distinctively Chinese, Indian, or Jewish. This is evident when Castoriadis says the 'solidarity' in other cultures can 'transform' or 'make fruitful' the heretofore existent, merely partial examples of autonomy (page 33). Finally, third, when Castoriadis speaks of 'only one' culture as recognizing the equality of cultures (pages 27-28), his phrasing, as he clarifies, ought to be read as referring to the autonomous aspect of Western culture; in other words, generally being a 'Westerner' would not suffice to make one a part of this 'one culture.' Hence, despite these awkward phrasings, Castoriadis's principled commitment to non-ethnocentrism should, I believe, govern the interpretation of these and similar passages. See also Gabriel Rockhill, 'Editor's Introduction: Eros of Inquiry: An *Aperçu* of Castoriadis' Life and Work,' in *Postscript on Insignificance: Dialogues with Cornelius Castoriadis*, trans. Gabriel Rockhill and John V. Garner (New York: Continuum, 2011), xxxix, n 91.

30. See Hannah Arendt, 'What is Freedom?' in *Between Past and Future: Six Exercises in Political Thought* (New York: Viking Press, 1961), 143–71.

31. See Jeff Klooger, '*Anlehnung.*' Furthermore, Greek democracy, even as an original creation, emerged *in* and *with* – and hence transformed but also preserved – social conditions that were already present and that stemmed from other cultures (see, for example, Castoriadis, 'Power,' 147–48). Thus, whatever one may think of the data and arguments of Martin Bernal, the basic idea that Greek culture draws on existing traditions – Egyptian, Sumerian, and so on – is obvious and this fact was acknowledged and even celebrated by many ancient Greek writers. See Martin Bernal, *Black Athena: The Afroasiatic Roots of Classical Civilization, v. 1, The Fabrication of Ancient Greece 1785–1985* (New Brunswick: Rutgers University Press, 1987).

32. See the discussion of this issue in Arnason, 'Castoriadis and Ricoeur,' 63.

33. See Castoriadis, 'Greek *Polis*,' where he says that in Greek democracy, whatever is of importance 'has to appear publicly. This is, for example, *effectively* realized in the presentation of the law: laws are engraved in marble and publicly exposed for everybody to see' (113, my emphasis; see also 87, 117). The qualifier 'effective' is essential and implies both the meaningful or cultural *and* the material or institutional levels of engagement. See also page 92, note 53, this volume.

34. See Castoriadis, 'Power.'

35. See page 75, this volume.

36. Sortition cannot guarantee democratic equality since a society might possibly commit to its use '*because* the founding fathers said so,' which implies heteronomy. Likewise, it would not be effective if it were used to abdicate decision when informed decision could be made in a fair way (see page 76, this volume). One would need to integrate sortition selectively and responsibly, along with other devices, into a larger autonomous political engagement.

37. See page 49, this volume. The emergent autonomy in these cities certainly 'leaned on' extant social-historical givens, which doubtless included remnants of Greek culture. The issue here concerns which remnants are attended to by the society, and *why*.

38. To avoid inadvertently advertising for them, I will not mention names. Suffice it to say that such movements can emerge anywhere to try and co-opt intellectual remnants of all kinds. On this ever-present danger, see also Umberto Eco, 'Ur-Fascism,' *The New York Review of Books*, 22 June 1995.

39. See, for example, Cornelius Castoriadis, 'The Retreat from Autonomy: Postmodernism as Generalized Conformism,' in *World*, 32–43.

40. See, for example, Cornelius Castoriadis, *Postscript on Insignificance: Dialogues with Cornelius Castoriadis*, trans. Gabriel Rockhill and John V. Garner (New York: Continuum, 2011).

41. See Castoriadis, 'Done.'

NOTE BY THE EDITORS OF THE FRENCH EDITION

Enrique Escobar, Myrto Gondicas and
Pascal Vernay

A transcription of this encounter by Nicos Iliopoulos was previously published in numbers 13 and 14 of *La Revue du MAUSS semestrielle* (1999). We reviewed a version that was corrected and completed by Jean-Louis Prat and introduced corrections of form into it, following the established practice for the publication of Castoriadis's seminars. We also reviewed and adjusted the original apparatus of notes.

INTRODUCTION

Jean-Louis Prat

The meeting between Cornelius Castoriadis and the *MAUSS* group (*Mouvement Anti-Utilitariste dans les Sciences Sociales*, or Anti-utilitarian Movement in the Social Sciences) may appear to have occurred both by necessity and by chance. It seems necessary in light of the sorts of questions raised by the *MAUSS* researchers and by the initiator of the journal *Socialisme ou Barbarie*. Yet it seems still more to have happened by chance, like the meeting mentioned by Diderot between Jacques the Fatalist and his master.[1] For this belated meeting, one Saturday in December 1994, does not have the convenient and conventional character of a university colloquium; and Castoriadis, before taking his place in what Bourdieu calls the 'intellectual field,' spent a long period in the universe of extreme left militants.[2] This was a subgroup situated at a great distance from the university milieus where *MAUSS* had been anchored since its creation. As its co-founder Alain Caillé tells it, *MAUSS* was constituted in 1981 after a colloquium on the theme of the gift.[3] In the course of the event he had remarked, along with Gérald Berthoud, that numerous contributors had been of accord in reducing the gift to a utilitarian strategy, even concluding that 'the gift does not exist.'[4] It seemed as if they were unaware of Marcel Mauss's thought and his famous *The Gift*.[5] It presents the gift as a 'total social fact' in which the dynamic of society is deployed and in which one finds expressed the triple obligation to give, to receive the gift (as a 'return of the favour'), and to surpass it with a counter-gift (in which the desire to 'save face' appears). It is an agonistic system in which prestige counts infinitely more than mercantile interests.

Even if the occasion served as a pretext and if, we may believe, something like *MAUSS* would have been born regardless, whatever the circumstances were, the anecdote justifies the way the acronym *MAUSS* invokes the memory of Marcel Mauss as part of the project of a critique of utilitarianism in the social sciences. This project of critique occurs *in the social sciences*, since it was shared by anthropologists, sociologists, and economists, though it was also bound to inspire *philosophers*, specifically readers of Alexandre Kojève and Georges Bataille such as Jean-Luc Boilleau or Jean-Louis Cherlonneix. These are thinkers who in their own works made conversant the agonistic gift, the Nietzschean critique of Platonism, and the desire for recognition.[6]

Readers of Castoriadis will find here the familiar theme that had played, and was still playing at the start of the 1990s, a role in his critique of Marxism. In a text cited below in the footnote, he mentions the Kwakiutl indigenous people 'who amass riches in order to be able to destroy them.'[7] This is the famous potlatch studied by Franz Boas, which served as the basis for Marcel Mauss's research. 'Some myopic "Marxists",' writes Castoriadis, 'scoff when one cites these examples, which they consider to be ethnological curiosities. But if there is an ethnological curiosity here, it is precisely these "revolutionaries" who have elevated the capitalist mentality into an eternal content of a human nature, everywhere the same.'[8] Yet Castoriadis's writing here goes back to the 1960s, to an era when Marxism was, for a master as well-known as Jean-Paul Sartre, an 'unsurpassable horizon.'[9] *MAUSS* itself emerged at the start of the 1980s, after the 'collapse of Marxism,' which was situated in the middle of the 1970s, according to the authors of *French Philosophy of the Sixties*.[10]

The Maussians, nevertheless, were not unaware of Marx, as Alain Caillé highlights in a text from 1997 entitled 'De Marx à Mauss sans passer par Maurras.'[11] He recounts that all those who

> were in the beginning and still are today the principal pillars and animators [of *MAUSS*] had a Marxist past. This was not a small-group Marxism, and it was one often more academic than properly militant, but there was nevertheless a Marxist past. And in a sense their adherence to a movement aligned with Marcel Mauss, while it consummated the definitive rupture with institutional Marxism, also signified a sort of fidelity to the Marxist ideas which had been their own.[12]

Notice that Castoriadis, by the time he had met up with *MAUSS*, had already long before broken in a very radical way with every form of Marxism, no matter how heterodox. This is perhaps not the case with *MAUSS*, since, according to Caillé,

> even if Marx was almost no longer cited or specifically commentated upon within its ranks, what characterizes the experience of *MAUSS*, in opposition to the majority of authors named above [i.e. Cornelius Castoriadis, Claude Lefort, Marcel Gauchet, Pierre Clastres, Guy Debord, Jean Baudrillard, and Karl Polanyi], is precisely its reticence to burn bridges with the central Marxian aspirations, i.e. its refusal to throw out the baby of radical hope – or rather the hope for a certain radicality – with the bathwater of totalitarianism.[13]

This indicates a divergence, even if one adds that,

> [There is] a connection to be clarified, namely that the Marxism *MAUSS* took as inspiration was a seriously revised one, i.e. one that was corrected, at once, by the tradition of thought that was developed by Claude Lefort and Cornelius Castoriadis, from *Socialisme ou Barbarie* through *Textures* and then *Libre*, along with Marcel Gauchet and Pierre Clastres, passing through the intensities of the *Internationale Situationniste* and of Jean Baudrillard, as well as through the humanist socialism and historical heterodoxy of Karl Polanyi.[14]

In the era of *Socialisme ou Barbarie*, Lefort and Castoriadis doubtless represented a 'seriously revised and corrected Marxism.' But each of them, following his own path, broke with the rationalist and determinist postulates of historical materialism by elaborating kinds of thinking that were no longer situated within the horizon of Marxism.

Even so, *MAUSS*'s Marxist connection could slip by unnoticed. After all, the critiques it formulated against 'utilitarianism,' the 'axiomatic of interest,' or also the 'explication of social practice through rational (economic) interests, which reigned supreme everywhere in the social sciences in the 1970s and 1980s,' could only cast

> a profound doubt over all that remains of utilitarianism in the heart of Marxism and, more specifically, over the explanation of history solely through the reality of material and economic interests. In the eyes of Marxists and orthodox materialists, nothing could appear more radically anti-Marxists than this refutation of the 'axiomatic of interest' as well as of its supposed capacity to explain social action positively and of its pretention to judge normatively.[15]

Alain Caillé presents this antagonism – between vulgar Marxisms and the heretics who called it into question – as an 'exacerbation of the tension that traverses Marxism between two ways of reading History in general and economic history in particular.'[16] This critique of 'orthodox' Marxism, even while it intends to remain faithful to the original inspiration of Marxism, calls to mind in many respects what Castoriadis developed in 1964 in 'Marxism and Revolutionary Theory.'[17] In that text he shows that despite pretty expressions like 'the emancipation of the workers will be the work of the workers themselves,' Marxism appropriated for itself the bourgeois conception of history and of society.[18] Its representation of history could only have validity for 'what happened during a few centuries in a tiny strip of earth around the North Atlantic.'[19] In effect, a theory that pretends to explain the history of human societies through the development of productive forces 'is not talking about history in general but only about the history of capitalism.'[20]

These few quotations seem to us to attest, if not to a perfect identity of viewpoints, at least to a very close proximity in the perception of the problems between Castoriadis and the Maussian researchers, whether anthropologists, economists, or sociologists. This proximity does not, however, exclude the existence of serious disagreements, which are expressed in the text that you are going to read, a transcription of a debate between Castoriadis and the members of *MAUSS*. These disagreements, moreover, also traverse *MAUSS*. On this point, Jean-Luc Boilleau recalled, during another debate where he represented *MAUSS*, that this was by no means a 'monolithic group.' He was pleased to attribute two popes to the church of *MAUSS*, i.e. the pope Alain Caillé and the antipope Serge Latouche, without excluding the possible appearance of an arch-heretic.[21] The subsequent meeting, which would happen three years later in December 1994, depicts these two as properly opposed to one another on themes of universalism and relativism, of direct democracy and the representative system, and concerning the very idea of an 'autonomous society' compared to a 'society against the State' as defined in the work of Pierre Clastres. Note that, on these themes, the pope Alain Caillé finds himself very close to Claude Lefort and Pierre Clastres, while the anti-pope Serge Latouche is more amenable to the positions of Castoriadis. Chantal Mouffe, it seems to me, defends the orthodoxy of 'political science' against the totalitarian slide she sees surfacing in direct democracy. As for Jacques Dewitte, who kept company with Castoriadis when they each collaborated for the journal *Textures*, his personal evolution, under the influence of Kolakowski and Levinas, distanced him so far from Castoriadis's theses that the idea of autonomy came to no longer even make sense to him. This is confirmed by a text he devoted to the thought of Levinas. There he describes autonomy as a 'form of freedom removed from all responsibility, [. . .] a permanent temptation of the West in its conception of freedom as pure autonomy, detached from every bond, released from all responsibility.'[22] It is embodied by the mythical figure of Gyges, a character he describes 'as an object of mistrust and reprobation: he is the very incarnation of a pure freedom detached from every bond, of an attitude of flight from his responsibilities.'[23] Like Ferry and Renaut in the book they dedicated to Castoriadis, i.e. *68–86 Itinéraires de l'individu*, he reduces autonomy to a 'process of emancipation of the individual with regard to traditions.'[24] He does not envision the collective autonomy of a community that institutes its *nomos*, its law, instead of receiving it from a transcendent authority.

But let us dwell rather on a previous debate in which Castoriadis participated, before the one that will occupy us here, but from which the popes of *MAUSS* were absent.[25] We are in May 1991 and the association of the Friends of the Librarie Sauramps – the major university bookstore in Montpellier – have organized a colloquium in the city on three grand themes: *Democracy as vio-*

lence? The end of history? In the East, another Europe? The choice of the three themes was of course tied to the questions that were sparked after the fall of the Berlin Wall about the future of a regime – 'the hardest and most fragile of regimes' as Castoriadis had said in 1982 – that Gorbachev was still trying to save by proceeding with reforms, the dynamic of which he could not control. These interrogations had already crystalized around the publication of a text by Francis Fukuyama, which sketched his famous thesis:[26]

> The transformations that are currently being completed in the Eastern countries, this apparent evaporation of the communist regimes, would signify not simply the end of communism but essentially the end of history itself; these transformations would imply the coming-to-awareness by humanity that there is nothing beyond the present society. The present society is the industrial, capitalist, and commercial society that constitutes our modernity.[27]

I am quoting here the summary offered by Jean-Claude Michéa for the Montpellier colloquium. It served to introduce the debate about 'the end of history' in which Cornelius Castoriadis, Edgar Morin, and Jean-Luc Boilleau would participate.

Jean-Claude Michéa began by recalling that for Fukuyama, 'to observe that we have entered into the end of history [. . .] is to understand – whether one rejoices or is saddened by it – that, with the last illusions now dissipated and armed with this new knowledge, there is nothing left to be done except to manage what exists.'[28] He then opened up the discussion of this thesis and formulated three questions:

> [1.] First Problem: As opposed to so-called traditional societies that aim (no matter the diversity of their forms) to maintain an

equilibrium, modern society has as an ideal and principle the positing of its own development as carried onwards to the infinite. Yet, can this disenchantment of the world – this growing submission of life to laws of economics – continue infinitely without meeting limits in the resources of nature, on the one hand, and in the patience of individuals, on the other hand? [...]

[2.] If this is not possible, and thus if, contrary to what Fukuyama thought, the critique and the surpassing of this world remains one of the practical necessities, does this mean – and this is the second problem – that the refreshing of Marxist critique (which remains the conscious or implicit foundation of the communist and socialist undertakings) would be enough to allow history to rediscover its genuine rhythm? Put differently, must we think that communism was not a digression in the century but simply a false start, i.e. that what was aberrant was not the essence of the project but only the historically determined forms of its implementation? Yet, doesn't suggesting this mean that one neglects to display what is *fundamentally common* – since Saint-Simon – to the imaginaries of communism, socialism, and capitalism, i.e. the almost religious belief in the necessity and possibility of an infinite development of large-scale industry?

[3.] Finally – and this is the last problem – it is obvious that these questions assume a philosophy of history. Is it, as Hegel and Marx wanted, the site of a dialectical, logical, and necessary development? Do the rise of capitalism and the Westernization of the world lie sleeping – in potentiality – in the Neolithic revolution or in the practices of the indigenous peoples of the Amazonian forest? Or must we, on the contrary, with Rousseau for example, rehabilitate the role of the contingent, of the accidental, all of which makes history an unpredictable adventure that puts into play the freedom of men, which means their aptitude to invent something new.[29]

INTRODUCTION

Jean-Claude Michéa is very close to *MAUSS*, and since he also passed through Marxism, we may observe that he is not happy just with the 'refreshing of Marxist critique' or with rehabilitating a 'heterodox' version of Marxism, since he refuses to blind himself to 'what is *fundamentally common* – since Saint-Simon – to the imaginaries of communism, socialism, and capitalism, i.e. the almost religious belief in the necessity and in the possibility of an infinite development of large-scale industry.'

As for Castoriadis's contribution at Montpellier, I would like to quote the last sentences of it, since they lead us to the questions that will be debated at the meeting with *MAUSS*, and they bear both on democracy and on the historical privilege of the societies in which it has appeared:

> All cultures have created magnificent works beyond the ensemblist-identitary kind.[30] But as for what concerns human freedom, there have been only two cultures, like two great flowers pushing up on the bloody field of battle, in which something decisive was created: Ancient Greece and Western Europe. This second flower is perhaps in process of withering away. Perhaps it depends on us for it not to wither away definitively. But in the end there is no guarantee that, if it withers away, a third flower might surge forth later, with more beautiful colours.[31]

In *The Imaginary Institution of Society* Castoriadis had already written that 'the Athenians did not discover democracy amidst the other wild flowers growing on the Pnyx.'[32] Democracy is not given by nature nor by the dialectical development of social relations. It is a historical creation and, as such, it involves chance. Nothing is more foreign to Marxist thought.

In Marx's thought, from 'On the Jewish Question' to *Capital* and 'Critique of the Gotha Program,' the foundational ideas of modern democracy are constantly reduced to the role of a juridical phraseology.[33] They constitute simply the formal conditions that make possible the generalization of commercial exchange. A commodity can only be sold and bought if its actual possessor, together with the acquirer to whom it will be transmitted, are free juridical subjects who dispose of one and the same *jus utendi, fruendi, et abutendi* with respect to the thing they are transmitting.[34] As long as the commercial sector remains enclosed in a feudal or 'Asiatic' society, the formal equality and freedom of the economic actors have not yet been elevated into 'natural,' eternal, and universal principles of the organization of society. But in modern capitalist society, wherein all the products of human labour and the labour itself become commodities, the juridical conditions for generalized exchange define the 'natural, imprescriptible, and inalienable rights' of man. The democratic ideology is nothing other than the conscious expression, seemingly rational, of the historical necessity that completes itself in the social relations of production. Yet it conceals the historical and contingent character of capitalist society and gives it the appearance of a 'natural' organization founded on 'human nature' and on the 'natural' laws of economics. According to the celebrated expression from *The Poverty of Philosophy*, 'There was history, but there is no more.'[35]

We should not underestimate the critical power of an argumentation that remains useful when one is faced with the ideological discourse of the liberal oligarchs, who continue to conceal the relations of exploitation and domination via the Noahic cloak of 'democratic values' and the 'rule of law.' This is, incidentally, the same approach that the young Castoriadis took, at the end of the 1940s, in rejecting the *juridical fiction* that, in the guise of Marxism, presented the USSR as a socialist state as soon as it had established the 'collective' property of the means of production. For the same reasons that drove Marx to deny the fictional equality that established the bourgeois right between employer and employee, Castoriadis denied the fictional appropriation of the social riches by the 'working class,' whose representation a single party had exclusively secured. Under different veils, the same exploitation was maintained as much in the East as in the West. It even reinforced itself in the way it deprived workers of the means for struggle, which they had been able to create through their previous struggles (unions, right to strike, workers' councils). It must be clarified, once again, that exploitation itself cannot be understood within the framework of a pretended *economic* science.[36]

In any case, this reduction of democratic principles to the ideology of the bourgeois class misrecognized the reality of fundamental freedoms that have nothing to do with the freedom of commerce, such as the freedom to communicate one's opinions, a freedom that one cannot enjoy unless all others enjoy it. If the freedom of the egoist and utilitarian individual '*stops* where the freedom of others begins,' then the freedom of the citizen '*begins* where the other's freedom *begins*.'[37]

On all of that, Castoriadis and *MAUSS* seem to be essentially in agreement. Yet, in the discussion Alain Caillé turns back against Cornelius Castoriadis the argument that he himself had brought against Marxism. If Marx was able to reduce universal history to a schema he drew from the recent history of Western capitalism, does Castoriadis, who presents democracy as a Greco-Western creation, escape from Hellenocentrism or Eurocentrism? Does he not misunderstand (contrary to the valuable observations of Pierre Clastres and, more unexpectedly, of Jean Baechler) the democratic character of ancient societies, which had the know-how to prevent the emergence of a separated power along with the schism of society into antagonistic social classes?

This objection assumes that democracy would be defined only by procedures such as election or sortition, to which one has recourse, quite naturally, in the societies where the site of power remains undetermined or where it remains an empty site, as with the Greek *agora*, where each person could take up speech in turn. As Jean-Pierre Vernant shows, it is in these conditions that democracy was constituted in Greece, when what is 'in the centre' of the city and social life was no longer the palace of the king, as in Knossos, but the public place.[38] Are these conditions 'necessary and sufficient'? If they are given, do they guarantee that democracy will bloom naturally, like a flower in spring? Recall that, among the Greeks, the most democratic institution, which was sortition, had at first been perceived as a means to allow the decision to be placed into the hands of the gods when men dared not decide for themselves.[39] But if, justifiably, we think the Greeks created democracy, it is because they took upon themselves the responsibility to give themselves laws that had been dictated to them neither by the gods, nor by destiny, nor even by nature.

This is something one cannot find, of course, in primitive societies, which remained dominated by immemorial traditions.[40] Democracy thus cannot be reduced to the indeterminacy of the site where legitimate power – and the legitimacy of power – establishes itself. After all, such an indeterminacy defines merely the 'open society,' in Karl Popper's sense, which means the liberal society. We certainly prefer it over fascism or Stalinism; but it is something completely different than democracy. In the debate with *MAUSS*, Castoriadis refuses to define democracy by indeterminacy – a term he leaves to Claude Lefort – and recalls that, for his part, he speaks of creation:

> As soon as we speak of the radical imagination in individuals and of the radical instituting imaginary in history – which is

what interests us here – we are obligated to admit that all societies alike proceed from a movement of the creation of institutions and significations. [. . .] Now, as soon as we no longer limit ourselves to considering history [. . .] but instead when we give ourselves the right to have political positions (and this is already to depart not only from philosophical consideration but also from the simple assertion of a *prima facie* equivalence of all societies), then indeed this right is not something self-evident.[41]

This is why, it must be said again, democracy is very much a historical creation of the Greco-Western world, which is not to say that it owns it like some good that must remain its own privilege. On the contrary, as soon as we adopt democratic values, i.e. those of a society in which as Rousseau says, 'obedience to the law one has prescribed to oneself is freedom,' then we posit them as universal values and we want them to rule over all society.[42] And yet, we cannot believe them to be 'natural,' in the sense that the law of gravity is natural. And since they are not natural, it would be false to say that they *are* universal, if one understands by this that they are by nature, forever before and after. Rather, they *become* universal; they are created by the instituting imaginary. Men – *anthrōpoi, homines, Menschen*, human beings from both sexes, and not *andres, viri, Männer*, men of the male sex – are not free and equal in rights; rather, we want them (him and her) to be so and hold to be inhumane the societies that treat them (him or her) as unequal, which is a judgement that applies to *our* societies. Through creating values, the Greco-Western man legislates for all men. But there is no question here of the imperial ethnocentrism by which one purported to impose 'civilization' on 'barbarian' peoples.

First of all, this is because the Greeks, in the classical era, never believed that they were more civilized than the Persians and the

Egyptians, whom they certainly called 'barbarians.' But this word, which appeared in Herodotus, was so far from having a pejorative sense that Plutarch, long afterwards, went on to write an essay 'on the malice of Herodotus,' whom he accused of being biased in favour of the barbarians.[43] It is only in the Roman era that the word 'barbarian,' in being applied to people who lived beyond the *limes* of the Roman Empire, took on the meaning that, later, beginning in the sixteenth century, came to provide a pretext for the colonial expansion of the Western world. This is what the progressivist intelligentsia believes itself to be denouncing when it repeats, following Lévi-Strauss, that 'the barbarian is, first and foremost, the man who believes in barbarism.'[44] But Lévi-Strauss himself, in a note added to the re-edition of *Race and History* (in his collection *Structural Anthropology, Volume 2*), recognized the logical incoherency of this shock phrase.[45] For in it 'the man who believes in barbarism' is qualified as a 'barbarian' by someone who claims one should not believe in barbarism. Montaigne knew how to avoid such an absurdity, in a text where he denounced European ethnocentrism, without falling into the trap of cultural relativism. In his essay 'On Cannibals,' he writes, 'I consider it more barbarous to eat a man alive than to eat him dead; to tear by rack and torture a body still full of feeling, to roast it by degrees, and then give it to be trampled and eaten by dogs and swine [...] than to roast and eat a man after he is dead.'[46] Montaigne does not call into question the existence of barbarism. He is satisfied to observe that the conduct of the Europeans is still more barbarous than that of the cannibals, who are certainly barbarous, 'by reference to the laws of reason, but not in comparison with ourselves, who surpass them in every kind of barbarity.'[47] This implies the reference to universal values, in the name of which a European can condemn the barbarism of his compatriots and render justice to colonized peoples. The word 'barbarism' no longer has to qualify a people as such but rather a manner of acting, aggressive or cruel.

These universal values are not to be confused with the values of our culture. They are universal only because they do not belong to us, *and because every man in every other culture is entitled to make them his own*. They are 'European' or 'Greco-Western' only to the extent, as Castoriadis explains in a text from 1983, that Europe no longer designates

> either a geographic entity or an ethnical entity. One of the strongest moments of the European creation is situated in New England at the end of the eighteenth century, and its effects have not ceased to be lively. And it [i.e. Europe] has not in fact been that way for two centuries. Japan, and the Democracy Wall dissidents in Beijing, and millions of people scattered across the planet belong to it. As for White South Africa, no.[48]

Europe, in this sense, is the society that claims itself as autonomous and cannot want to impose autonomy on men or peoples who are satisfied with being heteronomous. People have no love for armed missionaries, and there is no question 'using arms to regulate disagreements with people who continue to say, "Adulterers must be stoned," "Thieves' hands must be cut off," and so on.'[49] Autonomy, as Castoriadis declares in another text, propagates itself 'like a virus or a poison'; it exerts a 'liberating contamination' that can 'corrode' the 'essentially religious' significations that dominate, among other cultures, Islamic cultures.[50] The 'superiority' of secular and democratic societies cannot be claimed unless it is as that of societies in which we can ask ourselves if our laws are just, or if we should change them, whereas such an interrogation has no meaning in a society in which it is imagined that the laws have been dictated by a god.

Even so, this interrogation can disappear in a postmodern universe in which the divine laws pass over into 'natural' laws, those of economics, of bioethics, or even those of a liberal credo that gives to the 'rights of man' the transcultural status of an eternal truth and thereby hides the extraordinary historical creation that was their invention. To combat this collapse into heteronomous thought, Castoriadis remains more relevant than ever.

To conclude, I would like to give my gratitude to Rafael Miranda, Jordi Torrent, and Juan Manuel Vera, who were at the origin of this work through the development of the project of a Spanish edition.[51] I revised the text of the debate for it, which was initially published in *La Revue du MAUSS* in its two distributions in 1999. Thanks also to Juvénal Quillet, *the last but not least*, who passed his recording on to me, which allowed me to complete the text and correct some errors.

NOTES

1. See Denis Diderot, *Jacques the Fatalist*, trans. David Coward (Oxford: Oxford World Classics, 2009). —Trans.

2. See Pierre Bourdieu, 'Intellectual Field and Creative Project,' *Social Science Information* 8, no. 2 (1969), 89–119. —Trans.

3. On 'the gift,' see page 84, note 2, this volume. —Trans.

4. Alain Caillé mentions the creation of *MAUSS* in his book *Critique de la raison utilitaire : un manifeste anti-utilitariste* (Paris: La Découverte, 1989). Gérald Berthoud, mentioned in this anecdote, was among the interlocutors to whom Castoriadis responded in *Fait et à faire, Les Carrefours du labyrinth V* (Paris: Éditions du Seuil, 1997), which attests, in any case, to the existence of links between Castoriadis and the members of *MAUSS* well before the meeting of December 1994.

5. See Marcel Mauss, *The Gift: The Form and Reason for Exchange in Archaic Societies*, trans. W.D. Halls (Abingdon: Routledge, 1990). —Trans.

6. See Jean-Luc Boilleau, *Conflit et lien social, la rivalité contra la domination* (Paris: La Découverte, 1992), with a preface by Alain Caillé; and Luc Marie Nodier (pseudonym of Jean-Louis Cherlonneix), *Anatomie du Bien : Explication et commentaire des principales idées de Platon concernant le plaisir et la souffrance, la bonne façon de vivre, et la vie en generale* (Paris: La Découverte, 1996). See also my review of this second book, 'Anatomie d'un mirage,' *La Revue du MAUSS semestrielle*, no. 8 (1996), 360–66.

7. Cornelius Castoriadis, *The Imaginary Institution of Society*, trans. Kathleen Blamey (Cambridge, MA: MIT Press, 1998), 26. See full quotation in note 20 just below. —Trans.

8. Castoriadis, *Imaginary*, 26 (translation modified).

9. See Jean-Paul Sartre, *Search for a Method*, trans. Hazel E. Barnes (New York: Alfred A. Knopf, 1963), 136. —Trans.

10. See Luc Ferry and Alain Renaut, *French Philosophy of the Sixties: An Essay on Antihumanism*, trans. Mary H.S. Cattani (Amherst, MA: The University of Massachusetts Press, 1990).

11. See Alain Caillé and Sylvain Dzimira, 'De Marx à Mauss, sans passer par de Maistre ni Maurras,' *La Revue du MAUSS semestrielle*, no. 34 (2009). An earlier, single-author version appeared as Alain Caillé, 'De Marx à Mauss sans passer par Maurras,' *Marx après les marxismes, tome 1*, eds. Michel Vakaloulis and Jean-Marie Vincent (Paris: L'Harmattan, 1997).

12. Caillé and Dzimira, 'De Marx,' 66–69.

13. Caillé and Dzimira, 'De Marx,' 67.

14. Caillé and Dzimira, 'De Marx,' 67. Retrospectively, *Socialisme ou Barbarie* may appear to be an 'anti-totalitarian' journal; yet nobody at the time used that word. The word 'totalitarian' was itself used there, though quite rarely, to describe the Stalinist regime; but it aligns badly with the Marxist problematic that dominated this 'journal of critique and revolutionary orientation' (as it presented itself). The group existed from 1949

until 1967; the journal ceased to publish in 1965. The journal *Textures* stopped publishing in 1976. I seem to recall that the subscribers, of whom I was one, were 'compensated' for its stoppage by being sent a book translated by Jacques Dewitte, namely Leszek Kolakowski, *L'Esprit révolutionnaire* (Brussels: Complexe, 1978). The journal *Libre* appeared between 1976 and 1980 in the form of volumes published twice per year in the collection 'La Petite Bibliothèque Payot.' Its stoppage was the result of a conflict between Claude Lefort and Cornelius Castoriadis regarding the latter's work *Devant la guerre* (Paris: Fayard, 1981). See Jean-Louis Prat, *Introduction à Castoriadis* (Paris: La Découverte, 2007).

15. Caillé and Dzimira, 'De Marx,' 67.

16. The quotation continues: 'The first, which constitutes the framework of canonized historical materialism, tends to foreground a crude and linear evolutionism, which makes the modes of production succeed one another in a rigorous order so that they end up necessarily in capitalism, which is posited as the moment of the revelation of the reality of egoist material interests, and thus as the truth of history. In this perspective, if socialism appears as a "superior mode of production," this is uniquely owing to the superior instrumental capacity (by means of rationality) that it is supposed to acquire through giving priority to public interest over private interest, thanks to the granting state control to the economy. The second way of reading, which *MAUSS* has certainly privileged (by leaning notably on the work of Karl Polanyi) over and even against the creeping economistic Marxism of the Annales School is the way of reading that, on the contrary, highlights the unprecedented historical singularity of the capitalist economy with regard to universal history and the relatively recent and ephemeral dimension not only of capital but also of "commercial categories." From this perspective, Marx is found to be basically rather close to Max Weber' (Caillé and Dzimira, 'De Marx,' 69).

17. 'Marxism and Revolutionary Theory' originally appeared in *Socialisme ou Barbarie* but also constitutes Part I of Castoriadis, *Imaginary*.

18. Castoriadis, *Imaginary*, 57. —Trans.

19. Castoriadis, *Imaginary*, 25. —Trans.

20. 'To say, in effect, that men have always sought out the greatest possible development of the productive forces, and that they encountered as an obstacle only the state of technology – or that societies have always been "objectively" dominated by this tendency and organized as a function of it – is to extrapolate abusively to the whole of history the motivations and the values, the movement and the organization of the current society, or more precisely the capitalist half of the current society. The idea that the meaning of life would consist in the accumulation and conservation of riches would be folly for the Kwakiutl, who amass riches in order to be able to destroy them. The idea of seeking power and command would be madness for the Zuni indigenous peoples, for whom making someone the chief of the tribe means beating him until the point that he accepts. Some myopic "Marxists" scoff when one cites these examples, which they consider to be ethnological curiosities. But if there is an ethnological curiosity here, it is precisely these "revolutionaries" who have elevated the capitalist mentality into an eternal content of a human nature, everywhere the same' (Castoriadis, *Imaginary*, 26 (translation modified)).

21. This friendly depiction of *MAUSS*'s two 'popes' is also recounted in Sylvain Dzimira, 'Antiutilitarisme et décroissance. Compte-rendu,' *La Revue du MAUSS permanente*, 11 August 2007. —Trans.

22. Jacques Dewitte, 'Indétermination et contraction, ou de l'anneau de Gygès à l'Alliance,' *Cahiers d'études Levinasiennes*, no. 2 (2003), 110.

23. Dewitte, 'Indétermination,' 112.

24. Luc Ferry and Alain Renaut, *68–86 Itinéraires de l'individu* (Paris: Gallimard, 1987).

25. The contributions from this event were gathered in Jean-Luc Boilleau, ed., *De la fin de l'histoire* (Paris: Éditions du Félin, 1992).

26. In the summer of 1989 Francis Fukuyama published an article entitled 'The End of History?' in the American journal *The National Interest*, no. 16 (Summer 1989), 3–18. This article was included as 'La fin de l'histoire ?' in the fall of 1989 in the French journal *Commentaire* 47, no. 3 (1989), 457–69. It was in 1992 that he published the work that

developed his controversial theses, namely *The End of History and the Last Man* (New York: Free Press, 1992).

27. Jean-Claude Michéa, 'Introduction de Jean-Claude Michéa,' in Boilleau, ed., *De la fin*, 59.

28. Michéa, 'Introduction,' 59.

29. Michéa, 'Introduction,' 59–61.

30. The descriptor 'ensemblist-identitary' (*ensembliste-identitaire*), sometimes shortened to 'ensidic,' is a technical term coined by Castoriadis that is often used to modify the terms 'logic' or 'ontology.' It borrows from the French term for sets (as in set theory), i.e. *ensembles*. Most generally it refers to those aspects of reality that are determined, determinate, or determinable, as opposed to what is intrinsically indeterminate or positively creative. See Jeff Klooger, 'Ensemblist-Identitary Logic (Ensidic Logic),' in *Cornelius Castoriadis: Key Concepts*, ed. Suzi Adams (London: Bloomsbury, 2014): 108–16. —Trans.

31. Cornelius Castoriadis, 'Intervention de Cornelius Castoriadis,' in Boilleau, ed., *De la fin*, 71.

32. Castoriadis, *Imaginary*, 133. —Trans.

33. See Karl Marx and Fredric Engels, *The Marx-Engels Reader: Second Edition*, ed. Robert Tucker (New York: W.W. Norton and Co., 1978). —Trans.

34. The Latin phrase refers to the right to use, enjoy, and consume. —Trans.

35. See Karl Marx, *The Poverty of Philosophy* (Beijing: Foreign Language Press, 1978).

36. 'Exploitation is a *political* idea. It presupposes that another society is possible and affirms that the present society is unjust. If one accepts society such as it is, all the expenses (the *categories* of expenses) that take place there are necessarily determined by its structure and are necessary for its continuation: food for workers as much as police, prisons, and so on. If society must exist and function as capitalist society, law and order are inputs just as (if not more) necessary for the construction of the total product as the force of labour is. There is no Egyptian economy without priests and the Pharaoh. If an Egyptian peasant or slave got the idea that

the Pharaoh and the priests were exploiting him, then that would mean that he would have conceived of the possibility of another institution of society and judged it preferable' (Castoriadis, *Devant*, 211–12). Castoriadis had already sustained this thesis in an unpublished article, which was supposed to have been part of 'Marxism and Revolutionary Theory,' and which one can now read in the collection of posthumous writings edited by Nicholas Poirier, i.e. Cornelius Castoriadis, *Histoire et création, Textes philosophiques inédits (1945–1967)* (Paris: Éditions du Seuil, 2009), 175.

37. Castoriadis, *Imaginary*, 92. —Trans.

38. See Jean-Pierre Vernant, *Myth and Thought among the Greeks*, trans. Janet Lloyd and Jeff Fort (New York: Zone Books, 2006), 206 ff. On the *agora*, see page 89, note 29, this volume. —Trans.

39. On the importance of sortition, see Cornelius Castoriadis, 'No God, No Caesar, No Tribune!,' trans. Gabriel Rockhill et alii, in *Postscript on Insignificance: Dialogues with Cornelius Castoriadis*, trans. Gabriel Rockhill and John V. Garner (New York: Continuum, 2011), 11–12. —Trans.

40. 'One finds heteronomy in primitive societies, in fact in all primitive societies, whereas one cannot truly speak of a division between dominant and dominated levels in this type of society. So, what is heteronomy in a primitive society? It is that the people firmly believe (and can do nothing but believe) that the law, the institutions of their society, have been given to them once and for all by someone else, by spirits, ancestors, gods, or whatever else, and that they are not (and could not have been) their own proper work [. . .]' (Cornelius Castoriadis, *Domaines de l'homme, Les Carrefours du labyrinth II* (Paris: Éditions du Seuil, 1986), 43).

41. See page 33, this volume. —Trans.

42. Jean-Jacques Rousseau, *The Social Contract and Other Later Political Writings*, trans. Victor Gourevich (Cambridge: Cambridge University Press, 1997), 54.—Trans.

43. Plutarch, *On the Malice of Herodotus*, in *Moralia*. —Trans.

44. Claude Lévi-Strauss, *Race and History* (Paris: UNESCO, 1952), 12. —Trans.

45. See Claude Lévi-Strauss, *Structural Anthropology, Volume 2*, trans. Monique Layton (Chicago: University of Chicago Press, 1983), 362, note 1. The note refers the reader to Raymond Aron's 'interesting discussion of this passage' in 'Le Paradoxe du même et de l'autre,' in *Échanges et communications: Mélanges offerts à Claude Lévi-Strauss, à l'occasion de son 60ème anniversaire (Tomes I et II)*, eds. Jean Pouillon et Pierre Maranda (The Hague: Mouton, 1970). —Trans.

46. Michel de Montaigne, *Essays*, trans. J.M. Cohen (London: Penguin, 1993), 113. —Trans.

47. Montaigne, *Essays*, 114. —Trans.

48. Castoriadis, *Domaines*, 107. At the time this text was written, the 'dissidents of the Beijing Wall' were those whose voices were heard as a result of the work of sinologist Victor Sidane, in *Le Printemps de Pékin, Oppositions démocratique en Chine, novembre 1978–mars 1980* (Paris: Gallimard/Julliard, 1980). The most well-known of them, Wei Jingsheng, who was imprisoned for a long time before being banished in 1997, was at the time calling for the 'fifth modernization,' in other words for democracy, against Mao's successors including Deng Xiaoping.

49. Cornelius Castoriadis and Daniel Cohn-Bendit, *De l'écologie à l'autonomie* (Paris: Éditions du Seuil, 1981), 106. This work transcribes the conference organized by Castoriadis at Louvain-la-Neuve on 27 February 1980.

50. Cornelius Castoriadis, 'The Greek and the Modern Political Imaginary,' in *World in Fragments: Writings on Politics, Society, Psychoanalysis, and the Imagination*, ed. and trans. David A. Curtis (Stanford: Stanford University Press, 1997), 103.

51. See Cornelius Castoriadis, *Democracia y relativismo* (Madrid: Trotta, 2007).

DEBATE WITH THE *MAUSS* GROUP

10 December 1994, Paris, France

Cornelius Castoriadis, et al.

THE RELATIVITY OF RELATIVISM

CORNELIUS CASTORIADIS: I have a shortcoming in this discussion, which is that I've followed your publications, but undoubtedly not with sufficient diligence or care. So you needn't be upset with me if at times I display a shameful lack of information about your positions. If ever I misrepresent them – though I don't believe I will do so – then it will be unintentionally.

Alain Caillé asked me how to prepare for this gathering. I told him that to avoid an introductory exposition, which is always too cumbersome (for the public in any case), it would be best to send me a number of questions, and that's what he did. There are two parts in the letter he sent me. The first is not really a question. He asks me to make an assessment of the *MAUSS* group: [*Castoriadis reads the letter.*]

> [It] is in this spirit that we invited Claude Lefort who, while rereading several texts in *La Revue du MAUSS* for the purpose

of drafting a short paper to celebrate our tenth anniversary, suddenly felt himself to be at a great distance from some of our proposals, and notably from those of my friend Serge Latouche. Since, he said, it would require too much time and too many pages to explain the reasons for his disagreements, I invited him to come and express them for the completely informal *MAUSS* group.[1] Perhaps you could take over from that initial debate, with which you were familiar I believe. This would immediately open up questions we could ask you.

There were some other questions that followed.

I would like to say just a few things about this. I have a lot of sympathy for *MAUSS*. I have a lot of sympathy for what you do and for your critical spirit. But I would never dare to make an assessment of you. What does pose a slight problem for me are the limitations that you would trace out, or that you do trace out, for the idea or for the significance of the 'gift' as the means, but also perhaps as the end-goal, of an institution of society.[2] After all, at the same time, the majority of you – in any case Caillé, in what follows in his letter – seem to defend very fervently the idea of the market. We'll return to this in the discussion. There's something not entirely consistent there, I think. Or else one would need to try to specify what the spheres of the market are and what the spheres of the gift are; and then perhaps we must try (but I would prefer to do this later) to deepen and criticize a bit this idea of the gift. I will say a few things about this momentarily.

I read the paper Lefort sent you; you ask me to say what I think of it.[3] I don't have a lot to say about it in fact. To speak entirely frankly, as is my habit and my nature, I think in Lefort's work there's a defence of democracy in general, or a theory of democracy, if you will. (I will say some things momentarily about my own position.) But what I do not see in Lefort's work, despite the note on the bottom of the page that you added to his text, is any kind of critique of contemporary society.⁴ And I'm at once both very resolute about that issue and very unpleasantly surprised. There are sentences like: 'Don't think that I'm an unconditional partisan in favour of modernity or contemporary society.'⁵ I don't know who is an unconditional partisan of it. Balladur himself undoubtedly isn't, since he says: 'Change is necessary.'⁶ But what does that mean? What do we hold against contemporary society?

As soon as we lay it out precisely in light of its implications – even if it's only in light of the genuine idea of democracy in its full potentiality – we see that there are things that don't line up. And this critique extends well beyond the traditional Marxist or similar critiques. There are new phenomena, phenomena that are more than unsettling. There's a kind of collapse; we could call it an implosion – like a building whose foundation is giving way – of contemporary Western humanity. It's imploding, and it's starting to lean like the tower of Pisa, but perhaps without the same resilience.

ALAIN CAILLÉ: Perhaps it's going faster!

C. CASTORIADIS: Yes, perhaps it's going faster. But that's not all. It's not with an eye to pragmatic considerations that we're critiquing the contemporary situation. That's a small aspect of the question and not all that important. We're critiquing it for principled reasons, which means this: What do we make of this society in which the main thing that concerns people is, for those who are able at least, getting rich and, for everyone else, surviving and wasting away. There's a real problem there. The discourse on democracy as indeterminacy is fine – or not fine, I don't know – but it's not my cup of tea.⁷ In the end, there's a fundamental contemporary situation that we cannot accept as is.

I will turn now to the questions. I don't know if there are any comments on that, or things we can talk about now?

JACQUES DEWITTE: You can warm us up a bit more.

C. CASTORIADIS: I will go on then, and I will raise the temperature a little bit by reading Caillé's letter. 'On the other hand – and I am speaking here in my own name – I must tell you that while I have always had sympathy for what you write and for the clarity. . .,' and so on,

> I am left a bit unsatisfied on the following points. First point: I do not comprehend well how you reconcile your affirmation that all cultures are equal with the claim that one among them is more equal than the others, i.e. the culture of Greek society.[8] Supplementary question: To what extent is modern Western culture its legitimate heir? And would it also be entitled to be more equal than the others? This links us directly back to the first debate on the Heideggerian-Leftist Third-Worldism of my friend Serge [Latouche]. [*Laughter.*]

With that, I think the temperature is already starting to rise. [*Laughter.*] But it's also rising for another reason: I'm a bit offended. Firstly, the reason is (given that these accusations of Hellenocentrism are still there) that I do not speak of Greek society exclusively. I talk about the movement of autonomy within the segment of universal history that is the Greco-Western segment. This isn't only about Greece; it's doubtless also about Western Europe, starting at a certain moment, probably in the eleventh or twelfth century. Second, I have always gone to great lengths to affirm that I don't consider Greek culture, or for that matter Western culture, even in its better features, to be a model for the rest of humanity or for ourselves in the future. I am simply saying that something does begin there. There's the germ of something.[9] What is this germ? Quite simply, to put it in its simplest expression, it's the calling into question of oneself. And that's what we're going to do, what we are already in the process of doing today. Caillé's question, 'Are you not Eurocentric?' is a Eurocentric question. It's a question that's possible in Europe. I don't see anyone in Tehran asking the Ayatollah Khomeini if he's Iranocentric or Islamocentric. Because that goes without saying. This critique of oneself begins in Greece. It's Herodotus saying that the Persians are infinitely better than the Greeks and that the Egyptians are wiser.[10] It gets taken up again in the West starting in at least the sixteenth century with Las Casas, Montaigne, then Swift, and then Montesquieu (I am thinking of the *Persian Letters*), and then the Enlightenment. This contestation, this calling into question of oneself, is for me what's essential in the contribution of ancient Greece beforehand, and in the West afterwards. This is what allows, for example, for there to be a political movement, i.e. one of true politics and not of *the* political, as is said today by a fashion that to me seems stupid.[11]

THE POLITICAL AND POLITICS

C. CASTORIADIS: The political is what has to do with power in a society.[12] As for power in a society, it has always been there and always will be there, i.e. power in the sense of decisions concerning the collectivity that take on an obligatory character and the non-respect of which is in some way punished, even if it's simply the 'Thou shalt not kill.' That's unless we're supposed to believe in the bad anarcho-Marxist utopia that one day individuals will act spontaneously in a social way; that there will be no need for constraint or the like; and that there won't even be a need to undertake collective decisions. Marx talks, for example, about the rational planning of men's exchanges between themselves and with nature.[13] Yet, who carries out this rational planning? It's men. Are they all in agreement miraculously? No. There's a minority, perhaps, or several. Must they follow the majority or not? Or does each fall back into a part of the continent and apply his own proper plan? But what could all that mean? Therefore, there will be decisions of a collective order. These decisions will impose on everyone. Which is not to say that there will have to be a State, but that there will have to be a power. But this power has always existed, as much here as there, for example in the primitive tribe, in Clastres' tribe, on the plateaus of upper Burma, in China.[14] Confucius grapples with it. What is he addressing? The discussion of the better ways to manage an existing power. These are counsels addressed to those who govern, saying that the good emperor is the one we talk about as little as possible, as we read in the *Tao Te Ching*.[15] This is *the* political. But this is not what concerns us.

On the other hand, the part played by the Greek world and the Western world is *politics*. This is politics as collective activity that aims to be lucid and conscious, and that puts into question the existing institutions of society. Maybe it does so in order to reconfirm them, but it puts them into question. By contrast, in the framework of the Pharaonic Empire, the Empire of the Maya or Inca, the Aztec or Chinese, or in Babur's empire in the Indies, there may be a question of knowing whether or not one should carry out such and such a war, whether or not one should raise taxes, or peasants' work duties, or the like, but there's no question of calling into doubt the existing institution of society.[16] So, there you have what constitutes the privilege of, say, Western culture (and let's no longer say Greek culture). And that's what concerns us today. It puts itself into question and it recognizes itself as one culture among others. And, therein, we in effect have a paradoxical situation: We say all cultures are equal. But it must be observed, as a first approximation or a first step, if you will, that among all these cultures only one recognizes this equality of cultures. The others do not recognize it. This is a problem that raises theoretical political problems and may come to raise practical questions.

As it happens, the present situation is entirely disastrous, and for the moment we perceive no opening. Ten or fifteen years ago, Colonel Gaddafi – he was called crazy, and maybe that's so – declared that the catastrophic deviation in universal history took place when Charles Martel stopped the Arab expansion at Poitiers and that what should be done now is to Islamize Europe. If we want to be Islamized, that's fine. Otherwise, what's to be done? And not only that. There's constant talk now about the right to intervene. In yesterday's *Le Monde* there was a protest emanating from an Italian Christian mission in Sudan. The local Islamist government, after having beaten, tortured, and crucified them, had executed four Christians (perhaps it was the heads of the tribe).[17] I don't know if it's necessary to enact the right to intervene. In any case it's not going to happen. But is it the case that, since cultures are equal, we have to give up denouncing these acts, all while we would not and do not give up denouncing the death penalty in the United States, for example? There you have it. There, we have all at once an intellectual problem, if I may say so, and a paradox. But we have to confront these things. And there's also a practical problem that we're spared from at the moment, but maybe we won't always be. Its consequences risk being very significant.

A subsidiary question arises on this point. To what extent is modern Western culture the legitimate inheritor of Greek culture, and would it also have the right to be 'more equal' than the others? I have already responded to this in part. I think that right now, even within this state of disrepair or collapse, nevertheless Western culture is more or less the only one within which one can exercise a contestation and a calling into question of the existing institutions. Doing so does not immediately get you marked, I would say, as an accomplice of Satan, a heretic, a traitor to the tribe, to society, and the like. To what extent is this culture the legitimate inheritor of Greek culture? Perhaps the question doesn't have an enormous interest in today's discussion, and moreover the response can't be simple. In one sense, there are very important parts of Greek culture that have been abandoned, and we may regret that. Regarding other parts, we can do nothing but rejoice at their absence, as with slavery, for example, or the status of women. With respect to the problem of secularization among the Greeks – and even though in the modern world this question is not settled – the fact is that they had a very bizarre attitude toward religion. It was in effect a civic religion, an appendage of the State, and not the reverse. And then, for all that, there's an intellectual opening in our times that's even greater than in Greece. But, in the end, this is not really a question with an immediate practical interest, even if it is of very great philosophical interest, and even if we'd be right to say that there is, specifically in the history of philosophical thought, a tangential path that gets taken – I would call it a derailing – with respect to the earliest Greek thought. But this tangential path and this derailing are already there in Plato. It's what becomes thereafter – to put it succinctly – a sort of rationalism or the like, which manifests itself as much at the philosophical, intellectual level as at the practical level. But, in the end, for it to manifest itself, other elements also had to intervene that were not there even in Plato.[18] It's really a very particular question. Anyway, I will stop here for this point.

A. CAILLÉ: Thank you. I believe there are already lots of questions. Perhaps we have a first debate to initiate on this? [*Silence.*] Since no one is jumping in, I would like to respond, since I'm still left wanting for more and still perplexed. Basically, it seems to me that you are defending, on the one hand, a position that I would call hyper-relativist (even if you didn't do so right now), by affirming that societies proceed, one and all, from the same arbitrariness, i.e. from the radical instituting imaginary.[19] And from this perspective, it's impossible to order them hierarchically. Therefore, they are all valuable. And, on the other hand, you are on the side of what seems to me to be a very radical universalism. After all, you affirm in a nearly unconditional way – and it's here that I would like to question you – the value of one cultural dimension among all the others, beyond all the others, namely that of self-questioning. And from this perspective of affirming this unconditional value of self-questioning, which is furthermore (to go back to the very start of your exposition) the unconditional value of accepting the radical indeterminacy of the social relation, you, accepting this unconditional value, say: This value could only be realized in a society, in a certain period of history, in the case of Greek society, in a moment of the history of Western Europe, eleventh-twelfth century...

C. CASTORIADIS: ... starting in ...

A. CAILLÉ: ... starting in the eleventh-twelfth century, exactly. And this is found nowhere else. The fact of this historical singularity must be accounted for.

This is what raises the question for me in two ways. There is, on the one hand, a question of fact that we could discuss. I think you are right about the acceptance of collective indeterminacy. One could find, I believe, even elsewhere than in the West, traces of the acceptance of the indeterminacy of the individual subject (those of Buddhism, of Taoism, and so on); but with regard to things at the strictly political level, I think you are right. Yet the question that I'm posing for you is perhaps not so much the question of fact, which we could discuss more, but the question of right.

Do what you will, I do not see how you are able not to valorize, not to accord an eminent value to this self-questioning, to the acceptance of this indeterminacy. And as soon as you accept this – which, by the way, seems legitimate to me in many respects – necessarily you must valorize and consider as more equal than the others, as superior to the others, the only society in history that places at its core the acceptance of indeterminacy. And all of your reasonings go in this direction, for that matter, since, as you said a bit ago, you show that in all the other societies – all the societies other than European society – horrendous practices unfold. You talk of slavery and the situation of women. . . . This goes so far that, departing from the acceptance of all the cultural values of all societies, you end up in fact with the condemnation of all the values of all societies, except those of Western society.

INDETERMINACY AND CREATION

C. CASTORIADIS: First of all, a remark on the word indeterminacy.[20] This term is not in any way my own. I reject it. I speak of creation.[21] And creation is not simply indeterminacy. With respect to indeterminacy, there is perhaps such a thing in the quantum world – I know nothing about that – and there is undoubtedly an indeterminacy in every human world. But what democracy accepts is not simply indeterminacy but also many other things. It accepts, it affirms freedom. It affirms the right of the majority and at a minimum the equality of opinions, without which the right of the majority makes no sense. After all, if Plato were right, if there were some people who know and others who don't know, then we would not take the people into account. And more generally, at the ontological level, what defines being is not indeterminacy; it is the creation of new determinations. And if there ever is a society that accords with my wishes, it will not be a society of indeterminacy. It will be a society that determines itself in another way, precisely in a way that allows for the calling of itself into question and so on. But this is a creation; it is a *law* of that society. To speak of indeterminacy is in my view to say nothing meaningful. We should speak of a creative imaginary, one that is instituting, which means determining. Here, we're talking philosophy. So, in this respect, from the philosophical point of view, I had to speak a moment ago of a paradox, a paradox that perhaps essentially boils down to the passage from philosophy to politics. As soon as we speak of the radical imagination in individuals and of the radical instituting imaginary in history – which is what interests us here – we are obligated to admit that all societies alike proceed from a movement of the creation of institutions and significations.[22] There are the creations of the Maya and the Aztec, those of the Egyptians, of the Greeks, those of the thirteenth- and fourteenth-century Italians, and so on, and ours today, and those of the Chinese, no matter which ones. So, at the philosophical level I want to reject historical determinisms and to reject equally, for example, a philosophy of history of the Hegelian type, with its hierarchy of societies that progress by always realizing more of Reason until there is a society that completes its reign. There's that, on the one hand. Now, as soon as we no longer limit ourselves to considering history (that is, to *theōrein*, to doing theory, i.e. theory in the profound, strong sense of the term; to watching the unfolding of human history; to trying to understand it; to trying to understand different societies), but instead when we give ourselves the right to have political positions (and this is already to depart not only from philosophical consideration but also from the simple assertion of a *prima facie* equivalence of all societies), then indeed this right is not something self-evident.[23]

For my part, what surprises me very often in these discussions – and I am not directing this at you – is our provincialism. We speak as if people have always taken political positions, have always gotten the right to discuss and to criticize their society. But that is a total illusion, the provincialism of a hyper-cultivated milieu! These things only existed for two centuries in antiquity and for three centuries in modern times. And even then they didn't exist everywhere: only on tiny promontories, on the Greek promontory or the Western European promontory. That's it. Elsewhere, they didn't exist. A traditional Indian or Chinese person doesn't consider the act of taking political positions – of judging his society – to be something self-evident. On the contrary, this seems inconceivable to him; he doesn't have the mindset to do it.

So, as soon as we give ourselves this right, we find ourselves also with the obligation to say: Among these different types of societies, what do we choose? Islamic society? The Roman Empire under the Nerva-Antonine dynasty, i.e. the golden age, at least for those who were effectively rolling in the gold? Should we reinstate the empire of the Nerva-Antonines? Why not? Well, no! But why? In the name of what? Precisely because – and this is again a paradox – the culture in which we find ourselves gives us the armament and the means to have a critical posture. By means of it we make a choice from among, say, present historical paradigms, or from among possible projects – projects rather than paradigms since, as I said earlier, there is no model. There is a project of autonomy, which has its germ in Greece and in the West, but which undoubtedly must also extend much further. At that moment, we are positing ourselves as political men – i.e. beings or *anthrōpoi*, not males – and we are saying: Look, we are *for* . . . , e.g. for the rights of man, equality between men and women; and we are *against* . . . , e.g. against vaginal infibulation and genital mutilation. We are against it. I am against it. So, I don't see where the contradiction is. I have never said that from the perspective of a political choice all cultures are equivalent, for example, that the slave culture of the southern American States, depicted so idyllically by Margaret Mitchell in *Gone with the Wind*, is as valuable as whatever other culture, from a political point of view. That simply is not true.

I don't know if my response satisfies you.

C. MOUFFE: With respect to what you just said: The conditions for the universalization of these values – of self-critique, of democracy – that you defend, what would they be? Because I believe they can't become widespread unless a series of cultural conditions are given. Thus, how do you see these values of Western origin becoming the dominant values in other cultures? What would your position be with respect to that?

C. CASTORIADIS: This is a practical question?

C. MOUFFE: Practical and theoretical at once.

THE CONDITION FOR THE UNIVERSALIZATION OF WESTERN VALUES

C. CASTORIADIS: At the theoretical level, the response would not be very difficult, since we can simply talk about Tiananmen in Beijing. Contrary to what certain people have said (or would wish), democracy does not make up part of the Chinese tradition. That's not true. There were movements, there was Taoism and other things, but that is not what we call democracy. The Chinese, some at least, go demonstrate at Tiananmen. One of them is there, in front of the tanks. He gets himself crushed advocating for democracy. What does that mean? It means there is really an appeal in these values, as there was in the countries of Eastern Europe – even though things are quite bastardized there (it's sad but true) – after the collapse of communism. What I mean is that, as soon as these values are realized somewhere, if only in a very insufficient and very deformed way as they have been and still are in the West, they exercise a sort of appeal over others, without there being, for that matter, a fate or a universal calling of people for democracy.

But if what you have asked me is, 'What do we do if the others persist?' – since this is, after all, the question – then the response is: We can do nothing except preach by example. Robespierre said, 'People don't love armed missionaries.'[24] As for me, I'm not for imposing by force some democracy, some revolution in the Islamic countries or in others. I'm for the defence of these values, for their propagation by example. And I believe – but this is another question – that if at present this, let's say, radiance has lost much of its intensity (things are indeed more complicated than that), it's in large part due to this sort of internal collapse of the West. The rebirth of fundamentalisms on Islamic soil or elsewhere – after all, in India there are analogous phenomena among Hindus – is in large part due to what one must well and truly call the spiritual failure of the West. Today, Western culture is showing itself, alas, more and more for what it is: a culture of gadgets. What then do the other cultures do? With an admirable duplicity, they take the gadgets and they leave out the rest.[25] They take the Jeeps, the sub-machine guns, the television as a means for manipulation – at least the wealthy classes do, who have the colour televisions, cars, and the like – but they say everything else is Western corruption, the Great Satan, and so on. I believe it's all due to, and is also conditioned by, the fact that the West itself has a less and less powerful radiance because, precisely, Western culture – and this is insofar as it's a democratic culture in the strong sense of the term – is weakening itself more and more.

Yet, let's return to your question about the condition for the universalization of these values. The condition is that others self-appropriate them. And there's an addendum here, which is entirely essential in my mind, specifically that to self-appropriate them does not mean to Europeanize. This is a problem I'm not in a position to resolve. If it is resolved, it will be through history. I have always thought there needs to be, not some possible synthesis (I don't like this word; it's too radical-socialist), but a common transitioning that would combine the democratic culture of the West (along with the steps that must be or should be to come, i.e. a true individual and collective autonomy in society) with another mode of conservation, recovery, and development of the values of sociality, which endure – to the extent that they have endured – in the countries of the third world. After all, there still are, for example, tribal values in Africa. Unfortunately, they manifest themselves more and more in mutual massacres. But they also continue to manifest themselves in forms of solidarity between persons. Such forms are practically wholly lost in the West and are miserably replaced by the Social Security system. Therefore, I'm not saying it's necessary to transform Africans, Asians, or others into Europeans. I'm saying it's necessary for there to be something that would advance onwards; and in the third world, or at least in certain parts of it, there are still some comportments, anthropological types, social values, or imaginary significations, as I call them. They could likewise get caught up in this movement, transform it, enhance it, and make it bear fruit.

SERGE LATOUCHE: I would like to jump back and return to Alain Caillé's question, in the end, since Alain in fact took up mine, in a certain sense. I find that your position is, at any rate, a bit radical concerning this stepping-back – or this capacity for a critique of self – in other societies. After all, the examples that you are using, you take them from contemporary reality, which means from societies that are Westernized and poorly Westernized. These are modernized societies, which means ones in which we witness, owing to their contradictions, what one could call a totalitarian closure of the mind. There nevertheless were in ancient societies, in the great societies, in China, or in India some important periods of philosophical discussion with universalist dimensions and cases of stepping-back. Now, I understand well that this critique of self, this stepping-back in relation to self, never attained the level it attained in the West. That's clear. But this point has its reverse side. Certainly, the West pushed farthest the idea of a universal humanity, through opposition to specific existing cases of tribal self-enclosure (which, by the way, were never a total self-enclosure). Certainly, the idea of a potentially fraternal humanity of equal or identical men and so on was never developed as far as in the West. But how did it develop, and how was it constructed? In a very particular way. What made men into a collection, a solidary ensemble, is precisely the fact that we defined a common enemy of this humanity, which other societies did not do.[26] And this enemy is nature.

As soon as we decided that man was 'master and possessor of nature,' we designated the victim, which gave solidarity to humans among themselves.[27] This victim was nature, the secrets of which it was necessary to mine and which, as Bacon said, one had 'to submit to our desires like a public woman' in order to draw out from it materially the condition for a universal fraternity.[28] This condition was the enrichment of everyone, which would thus allow for eliminating the conflicts between men, transferring them into conflicts between men and nature. Therein lies, potentially, this contradiction whereby through instrumentalizing nature – which previous societies or other societies had never done to this extent – we gave ourselves the means to instrumentalize man per se. If, within the same movement, we proclaimed a universalist fraternity, we also destroyed it through deciding that certain men were not men, or were sub-men. They were transitioned over, qua slaves, to the side of nature. And thus, we could just as well subjugate them and treat them according to our desires. All of a sudden we perhaps abolished slavery, but we invented the concentration camps.

C. CASTORIADIS: I have no problem with, so to speak, softening to an extent the edges of an opposition I present as sharp, given that I want to highlight something. I want to shake people up. I want to make it understood that man is not, by divine right, a democratic being; that democracy was a creation and a conquest of history; that it's constantly in danger; and that furthermore it's in process of going away. In Europe we had totalitarianism and we have, after totalitarianism, the power of the corrupt media, politicians, and big businessmen.

But, first of all historically, it's no doubt necessary to step back and examine more closely the case of India and of China. It's not only that self-questioning was pushed much less far along at the intellectual level. The two points are indeed entirely conjoined. It's also that this philosophical culture remained a culture of the mandarins, in the broader sense of the term. It doesn't take place in the *agora*.[29] It takes place in a closed milieu, which is the milieu of well-read people, the sages, the philosophers, and the like. This is true as much in India as in China. And, tied in with this – and this is obvious to me – you never see in India nor in China this combination of restlessness and the movement of philosophical interrogation with the political question. Take the greatest sages. You see them saying: The emperor X should do this or that. In other words, it's a matter of the reasonable management of the instituted power. For example, never does a radical utopia emerge – even though one may criticize the idea of a radical utopia – from the pen of a philosopher, one concerned with the state of the city, of the society. That's the first point. Otherwise, I'm entirely in agreement with you in accepting the idea that in Buddhism, or indeed in Taoism, there is a calling-into-question that goes pretty far, to the level, once again, of representation, of the representations of the tribe.

Now, when you say that in the West universality was gained at the expense of an enemy that is nature, and that the instrumentalization of nature transformed itself into an instrumentalization of humans, I would say: yes and no. Why? I'm entirely in agreement with you in saying that a new attitude with respect to nature appeared in the West and, contrary to Heidegger by the way, I don't think it's the result of Western metaphysics. I think that the journey taken by Western metaphysics is, starting at a certain point, correlative to – without in any way being the result of or the reflection of – the journey taken by all of society. There's an imaginary of rational mastery that appeared in the West, indeed before Descartes and even before Bacon, with the Swiss watchmakers at the end of the Middle Ages, when a precise measure of time was needed.[30] And this factor isn't necessarily tied to the others; it doesn't, in itself, constitute progress of the productive forces. It's also a will to lay down order. There's Bacon. There's Descartes: 'masters and possessors of nature.' There's Leibniz: 'While God calculates, the world emerges,' and so on.[31] There's this whole movement and also, of course, the idea that one can and must exploit to the maximum a nature that's there as a simple object of exploitation.

You doubtless know that I'm entirely opposed, including politically, to that attitude. But I would say that it's not necessarily bound up with what I call the Greco-Western movement towards autonomy. For example, that attitude is in no way characteristic of the ancient Greeks, absolutely not. There, the connection with nature is completely otherwise; the trees are inhabited by the dryads, the rivers are gods, and so forth. Here, we are dealing with the question of the relation between the movement towards autonomy and capitalism. There's in effect something very important, very strange, that unfolds in the West starting in the fourteenth to seventeenth centuries. This is the coexistence of two nuclear imaginary significations. On the one hand, there's the movement towards autonomy. On the other hand, there's capitalism, briefly put. They seem more or less to join up around the idea of rationality. This is a historical misunderstanding, if I may say so, if the term 'historical misunderstanding' has a meaning, and if one can accuse history of generating misunderstandings. But, said Baudelaire, 'The world only goes round by misunderstanding.'[32] And this misunderstanding likewise manifests itself in the seventeenth to nineteenth centuries in, for example, the adoption of a certain number of ideas – of orientations – that are squarely capitalist by the workers' movement and particularly by Marx, among others. (Marx is non-synonymous with the workers' movement, of course).

One last point about this: I also do not think that the instrumentalization of nature is what drives towards the instrumentalization of humans. I think the two proceed from something else, namely from the idea, the imaginary signification, of an unlimited expansion of rational mastery. The instrumentalization of humans, in the form of slavery for example, can be found independently of capitalism, independently of ancient Greece. Ancient Greece was not exceptional in having slavery. All ancient societies were familiar with it, including the African societies, as we know very well. Thus, it's something else, I think. What must be said is that in previous societies the exploitation of nature, like that of humans, emerged, if I may say so, in a naïve way. That is, one would chain someone up and make him work, for example. And in capitalism the one and the other, the exploitation of nature and the exploitation of humans, are done with chronometer in hand. You must do so many acts in one hour of work and so forth.

I don't know if you're satisfied with my response.

JACQUES DEWITTE: I have two questions to pose, but I'll reserve the second one for later because it is more general. The first, a remark, came to me while listening to you there when you said that, at bottom, this is not about Europeanizing. Thus, you supported the idea that it would be desirable, ideally of course, to maintain certain tribal values, for example the idea, the practice, of a solidarity. Now, while listening to you, I'm saying to myself: But doesn't all this bring us back to ourselves? Isn't it also valid for ourselves? In the end, wouldn't there be a danger in thinking of ourselves, in comprehending ourselves purely, essentially, as self-questioning beings, i.e. beings who put themselves into question by themselves, but forget that there is something else in our identity, in what we are, in our tradition, and that there are also values of solidarity. I believe we call that, here in the *MAUSS* group, 'primary sociality.'[33] Thus, it seemed to me that this brings us back to ourselves.

A. CAILLÉ: May I add a little complement to Jacques Dewitte's question? You're calling for the combination of the values of self-interrogation with those of solidarity, i.e. of a general sociality, which is more alive elsewhere than here. But the formidable question is really that of knowing to what extent these values of solidarity are partly bound, if not to the repression of, then at least to the shutting out of the values of self-questioning.

C. CASTORIADIS: Since, with Lefort, you're talking above all about Tocqueville, I will send you back to Tocqueville.[34] For him, under the Ancien Régime, there was this social chain going from the most poor of the peasants, and actually from the serfs, up to the monarch. There were solidarities. The noble was not only or not essentially the horrible exploiter, dominator, and so on. He was also the one who took care of his men and everything else. The village had solidarity. For Tocqueville, all of that got dissolved – or tended more or less to get dissolved – in the movement towards the equality of conditions. That's entirely true. But the question is: What do we do now? In the West, these values were lost or are on their way to being lost. Short of making a long parenthetical aside or telling my life story, on a Greek island where I always go to pass the summer, every year I witness – I can see it as if on a thermometer – the growing dislocation of the villager community, which was still very alive fifteen years ago. Fifteen years ago, every year, a family was responsible for the village festival and prepared the great collective Christmas feast that happened beside the church. Through all of that and through a whole series of other things, the village was alive. I did a quick calculation. It was – how to say this? – living off 97 percent self-production and self-consumption. It imported iron and silk, that's all. All the rest was produced, built, cultivated, woven, recycled, or the like in the village. And all of that is in process of breaking down, if only because there's no more village. The people are not leaving for Germany or Australia but for Athens. What can be done there?

If there's a striking thing in politics, it's in noticing – when we are not being superficial, and I hope not to be – that the citizen is not, must not be, and cannot be, if he's a true citizen, a disincarnate being. A political consciousness is not what puts itself into question, what calls into question what surrounds it. A human being does that, i.e. one who belongs to a community and so on. And this community has values that are neither philosophical nor political as such. They are partly aristocratic values but above all the values of human life, like those we are alluding to here. And these values can't even be formulated, even less so imposed, in and through a political program. What can we say about this? When I first came to Paris, Bastille Day was already there, and I danced every night in my neighbourhood, at Rue Falguière, at Metro stop Pasteur.[35] Every bistro put on its own ball. Each had its little band, the accordionist, and everyone from the neighbourhood. Bastille Day would come and we started on the afternoon of the thirteenth and wrapped up on the fourteenth, late at night, eating sandwiches, dancing, above all to the bal-musette style but also at a certain point to the rumba, the samba, and the like. And since the sixties that no longer exists. Paris no longer exists. There were neighbourhoods. There aren't any more. What do we do now? Do we inscribe into a political program the reconstruction of the neighbourhoods of Paris as urban villages with Bastille Day, the corner grocer, and everything else? I'm absolutely sorry for the evolution of Paris. But what's at stake is an authentic, informal creation of society which is now ruined. One may have hope for it, i.e. that it will restart; and doubtless it will restart in other forms. But we can't lay it out in a political discussion unless it's just to note that, effectively, there's a problem there.

J. DEWITTE: So, this is the acknowledgement of the limits of our power to act?

C. CASTORIADIS: Absolutely. We are not the society. We are a constituent of it in a prospective social movement. And we can thus also say, like Caillé, that there are values of solidarity that are very important. But we cannot make it into one of the points of a political program.

S. LATOUCHE: Just before, I didn't immediately react to your response. But I care to return to it. It doesn't satisfy me fully because you dissociate the three elements that for me constitute a sort of whole in my analysis, namely rational mastery, the domination of nature, and humanism. First of all, I think that these three elements are already there in germ form in the Greeks. There's no radical break in the history of the West between antiquity and the Renaissance. And, furthermore, we don't find those elements anywhere else. When you say there were slaves not only in the West, that's true. But the category of 'slave' gathers extremely different things, extremely different attitudes. A 'domestic captive' in Africa counts as a slave, since they could make him into a slave through the slave trade, but that's not the same as a thing. He counts neither as an instrument nor a thing. He doesn't count entirely as a man, since when they're not a member of the tribe, they're not completely counted a man. But the animals aren't men either and, for all that, they aren't things. They too make up a part of the universe, of the cosmos, and so forth. So, this is entirely different. Yet, precisely, it seems to me that this attitude is already changing in ancient Greece. You mentioned the dryads, but I don't think Aristotle believes much in the dryads, and in his era. . . . There are texts of Aristotle – obviously you are a lot more competent than me on this; my mastery of Greek is very limited. There's a text where he says, if my memory is correct, that there's no place in the city for horses, for other animals, for things, and so on. He says there's no *philia* possible between man and horse.[36] There's indeed a rather radical exclusion of nature, which didn't exist in an African animist society. And, in effect, Greek and Latin law thus already go on from there to define the slave as an *instrumentum vocale* and thus make possible an instrumentalization. So, there's already a beginning there. And it's not by chance if at the same time in Stoicism the humanist ideology appears, i.e. the idea that there exists a common interest of humanity. And what is the common interest of a humanity divided into tribes, into religions, into nations, or the like, unless it's that all men have in common an interest in becoming dominant over AIDS, in mining into the secrets of nature, in mastering the universe, and so on? As soon as this idea of a common interest takes shape – of a humanity against nature – this category of humanity can appear. It thus appears with this Western universalism, let's admit that. But it appears with these two components, which, in my view, we cannot dissociate.

C. CASTORIADIS: Perhaps we shouldn't prolong this discussion since, here, we're entering into a terrain that's very complex, very difficult, and very slippery, specifically that of the relation between real history and the evolution of ideas. And, personally, I'm quite opposed to the idea of reducing real evolutions to ideas or of making them correspond to them, i.e. this species of inverted Marxism, which is Heidegger's little indulgence by the way. It holds that Western technocracy is the completion of Western metaphysics, and so forth. Well, that's not true. Thomas Aquinas is a grand metaphysician, but he has nothing to do with rational mastery and the world of technology.

I don't agree with your historical analysis. I believe that an entirely particular turn is taken by the West starting at a certain moment. I don't think the situation is the same in antiquity. Slaves can be freed, and a lot more in Rome, as you know, than in Athens. In late antiquity there were even emperors, in the third century, who decreed collective emancipations. In the history of slavery, Aristotle is a particular case. To my knowledge – and no one has changed my mind yet on this topic of discussion – Aristotle is truly the first Greek who justifies slavery.[37] Plato doesn't justify it, nor does anyone else. And Aristotle does it with restrictions, for that matter, since when he speaks of slaves by nature, he offers a definition that one could almost accept. He says that these are people who are not able to self-direct themselves. But we put the people who are not able to self-direct themselves into the psychiatric hospital. And we mustn't forget that the Greeks became Greek. They learned to read and write with Homer; they chanted Homer at the festivals. Yet, in Homer there are characters of whom one knows in advance that they're going to become slaves. And who are they? They're the noblest characters in the epic. It's Andromache, for example. And you can see in Thucydides, in the discussion of the Athenians and the Melians, that there's no attempt to make a rational justification there.³⁸ The Athenians say: This is a law we didn't invent; we found it there; and it is valid among humans and among gods. The law is the right of the strongest. It's Aristotle who had the idea, as a philosopher, to rationalize this state of things and to say: No, it's not just Andromache; there are lots of people who are slaves by accident and shouldn't be so.³⁹ So, I think this is something that changes with modern capitalism. It changes even regarding the relationship to slaves, insofar as they continue to exist in the Western hemisphere at the start of the nineteenth century. They exist in the slavery – quasi-slavery – of the industrial proletariat, in what we rightly called the reification of work, which is something quite different than before. And the idea of humanity does not go along with the idea of rational mastery. Here, we are getting into extremely complicated discussions. For example, the idea of humanity is that of the Stoics, of course, who nevertheless drew from it no practical conclusion, as you know, since for them there is no question of political action. But that's also the Christian idea. That's Saint Paul: 'There is neither Jew nor Greek, slave nor free, man nor woman.'⁴⁰ This idea, as an idea, is there for fifteen centuries; as a reality, it is not Christianity. Contrary to what the clerics say, Christianity never raised a finger to abolish slavery. And when Las Casas defended the Native Americans by saying, 'No, they have a soul,' it was in order to say at the same time, 'No, the Africans have no soul, so you can subjugate them and transport them to the Americas.'⁴¹ I think that of course these ideas play a role in history, but they are the expressions, the results. They can become the motors anew when they are taken up into historical evolution. For example, the Western Europeans are somehow Christianized during a very long period, but it's only in the fourteenth century that the peasants rise up in England and start singing, 'When Adam delved and Eve span, who was then a gentleman?'⁴² This idea had been there since the year sixty after Jesus Christ. No serf, no slave used it yet. But when the historical situation changed, when society started to protest, it took up Christianity and made something else out of it. And this Christianity that preaches equality down here on earth is not a true one. Christianity preaches equality up there on high. My response is a bit diffuse, but I believe the question itself is diffuse. Not your question, the question, *die Frage*, the problem.

A. CAILLÉ: One final question, perhaps, on this point? Louis Baslé?[43]

LOUIS BASLÉ: These are above all remarks; it's neither agreement nor disagreement. But the Hebrew question is never broached, and monotheism seems a very important element in the idea of humanity, just as in, I would say, the Judeo- or Hebraico-Greek convergence. You cited Saint Paul. There are some things there, some rather interesting points of bifurcation that can sleep for centuries. That's a first point. Here's another one. I think that, despite yourself, you're not as far from Lefort as you say, and that at the same time you two are in radical opposition. As soon as you talk about the possibility for contestation, you have indeterminacy, there's nothing to be done about that. And when you move from a world of aristocratic warriors to a mass democracy, well then you automatically have decadence, privatization, abdication, all of which Tocqueville rightly analysed. You get the fact that, instead of forming a community, one forms a society, as Baechler says in his latest book.[44] At that moment, the political will subsides, quite obviously, and the scene gets occupied, we might say, by communities of interests. All that is well understood; it's what you were talking about just a while back. So, at that point, it seems to me that this pertains more to a positive sociological description. In other words, there are social mechanisms that will get set into place automatically and a certain number of referents, of principles, of calibrations are there, I would say. And, at that point, this means: It's not because you have a radical, self-critical imaginary and so forth that you've thus forgotten about the forces of power, the forces of the social, or the like. They're treated differently in your society, in particular the invisible and all such things that get talked about very little. The fact of emancipating oneself from the invisible goes back to Tocqueville's and to Rousseau's question, to everything you've also brought up. And regarding that, I believe democracy is called to die and to be reborn, which seems to me to be something enshrined, I would say, in the very flow of the evolution of social systems. I have a sort of radical pessimism, or a radical optimism, in the sense that it's reborn, restarts. But I think there's an entropy of democracy, i.e. that it leads to the emergence of a mass. This makes it such that it self-destructs, as Baechler said, sometimes at the hands of the clerics, curiously, and not necessarily due to the masses or through corruption, which might be in play as well. So, that's all.

C. CASTORIADIS: I'm not going to revisit the question of monotheism. You've said what's essential. Whatever its importance was, the ideas relative to these questions remained dormant for centuries. Thus, henceforth we have to ask ourselves: Why the devil were they reawakened at a given moment in time?

L. BASLÉ: You're doubtless thinking of the revival of Greek antiquity.

C. CASTORIADIS: It's before the revival of antiquity, it seems to me. I link this to the proto-bourgeoisie, to the constitution of free cities in the West (which we will come back to sometime), to the attempts at self-government in opposition to the central power and the luck they had in navigating between the king, the pope, feudalism, and so on. With respect to the question of contestation and of indeterminacy: yes and no. After all, if you will, indeterminacy for me... how to say it? As soon as I begin to talk about the radical imagination and the radical instituting imaginary, which means a spontaneous creativity proper to human beings, it becomes obvious that there is indeterminacy, and this indeterminacy is everywhere. It was there in imperial China, it was in Stalinist Russia, and so on. But when exactly does it take on an actual substance? As soon as one exits from heteronomy. This is what you call the emancipation from the invisible. Yet, traditional societies are mythico-religious societies, or purely and simply traditional ones for that matter, and not necessarily religious in the proper sense of the term. In them, precisely speaking, there's no question of contesting the social law or the representation of the world created by the society. After all, those things are seen as a gift from the invisible, or as an imposition, a law of the invisible, or the like. And from this perspective, modern society contrasts sharply with all the others. Greek society occupies a particular position, not because it was a secular society – it was not – but, as I said a moment ago, because the religion there was civic religion (thus anticipating in a way Rousseau) and because it made up part of the functioning of the city. The Greeks, by the way, while being very pious most of the time, never dreamt for example of sending people to the Delphic oracle to ask, 'What laws should we make?' They did, however, send emissaries to the oracle to ask all sorts of questions, even, 'Where should we establish a colony?' But not, 'Is this law, or that other law, good?' In other words, legislation was outside the domain of religion. Political society was outside the domain of religion. Now, is it such that as soon as there's democracy there's a mass formed, privatization, the gravity of power, and so on? Here, we diverge about the sociological observation and the like. I don't think those things are fated, and I don't think, in particular, that they're tied to the democratic composure of modern societies. This too is a very complicated discussion. There was a moment of struggle culminating in the revolutions against the Ancien Régime at the end of the eighteenth century and even in a large part of the nineteenth. There was a collective participation in political combat, and democratic regimes were established in Europe as a function of popular struggles. These popular struggles were the struggles of the people. They were also the struggles of the petite bourgeoisie, since they, and not only the intellectuals, played a very important role in all the countries. It's true that starting at a certain point in time you have a retreat of the population, which I have referred to since 1960 as privatization.[45] But to say that this retreat is due to the democratic composure of this regime and that it was foreseen more or less by Tocqueville – recall that Tocqueville didn't observe it but made a prediction, since in his era it wasn't true – would be erroneous in my opinion. A whole series of factors trended at the time in the direction of a disappearance of the project of autonomy. The movement towards the extension of democracy, in particular in the social and economic domain, came to a halt at a certain point. There was also the role of Marxism. There was the expropriation of the popular labour movement by it. There was the evolution of parties claiming to adhere to Marxism (even if they were divided starting at a certain point between social-democracy and Bolshevism, in both cases with catastrophic effects). And there was the bureaucratization of the labour movement. But the bureaucratization of the labour movement is not a phenomenon of democratization. That's completely an opposite thing. That's the expropriation of what in the beginning could have been a power, i.e. a control by the workers' collectives over the organizations, as with the first English syndicates, for example, and in other places too. That's the transition into bureaucratic organizations and the cornering of the power by the bureaucracy. Add to this the evolution we saw with Bolshevism; the experience of the communist parties; the schism in the labour movement; the conviction held by a large part of the working class that there was a paradise over there and that there were leaders who knew everything; the conviction held by another portion of the working class that it was a hell over there and that the Bolsheviks were emissaries of the devil (which was the situation in the Anglo-Saxon countries, in the United States for example). Hence, there was a collapse of the forms that could have appropriated the project of autonomy at just the moment when they wanted to carry that project beyond the narrowly-defined political sphere, the sphere of rights, the right to vote, and so on. This factor combined with the capitalist movement proper, which means, say (the exact terminology is unimportant), consumer capitalism. This is a species of strange dialectic through which the workers imposed on the capitalist regime an elevation of the standard of living by way of imposing an enormous enlargement of the interior market, without which capitalism would have doubtless collapsed, as Marx had thought. And starting from that moment, with no conspiracy nor any conscious act, there was the explicit adoption by the capitalist regime of a politics of the enlargement of interior markets. And thus there were agreements to augment salaries, from which, if we throw in the lethargy and the collapse of the combative dimension, flowed the turn of the population towards consumerism, television, and so on. I believe this is a sociological evolution that is very, very complex. And I absolutely do not agree with blaming it on the egalitarian ideology, in Tocqueville's sense.

DEMOCRACY

A. CAILLÉ: We're going to move on perhaps to the second question.

C. CASTORIADIS: Yes. [He reads Alain Caillé's invitation letter.]

> Another question, namely that of democracy. Here too I find you to be a bit too Hellenocentric. If democracy only ever

existed in Athens, that's because it represents a political regime too improbable to be worth the effort of fighting for. What do you think of Baechler's theses concerning the naturalness of democracy?[46] Is there perhaps a Berber, Iroquois, or other democracy, or instead do the Greeks have the exclusive monopoly on it?

First of all, the Greeks do not have the exclusive monopoly, since there are also the Western Europeans and the North Americans. There's no question of Hellenocentrism. Second, I disagree entirely with Baechler's theses, which I consider to be completely far-fetched; but I don't want to talk about them. I don't believe there would be a naturalness to democracy. I believe that there's a natural slide of human societies towards heteronomy, not towards democracy. There's a natural slide into looking for an origin and a guarantee of meaning elsewhere than in the activity of humans, for example in transcendent sources, or among ancestors, or in Hayek's version of it in the divine functioning of Darwinism across the market, which makes it such that the strong and the better always prevail in the long run, which is the same thing.[47]

Is there some democracy among the Berbers? I directed a thesis on this people group that will be defended on Thursday. I don't think one can speak truly of a Berber democracy. That's a French ideological mirage from the end of the nineteenth century, bound up with the needs of colonization. They contrasted the Berbers, who were presented as true Europeans, with the Algerians. They even said the Berbers have the same heads as the Auvergne inhabitants, and their houses are built in the Auvergne style! They found in all of this a good basis for the French colonization of Algeria. Doubtless there was, if not a democracy, at least a collective power among the Iroquois, among other indigenous peoples, among the Zuni, at least if one believes Ruth Benedict.

But what makes the difference? I believe that the difference with Athens, with Western Europe, is that in the case for example of the Iroquois or the Zuni, we're faced with something that's traditional, inherited, something that's simply there. It's the law of the tribe. It's not something one need change. The law of the tribe is that the collectivity exercises the power. Apart from that, there's nothing to change. In the tribes described by Clastres, the chief has a decorative role. He's like a tape recorder reel that repeats, 'This is what our ancestors have laid down as law; it's the law of all, and it's a good law.' The role of the chief is to chant that from morning to night, like a cockatoo could have done if someone had taught it to him. In short, there's no true leader.[48] But there's no putting things into question. There's no idea that the law comes from the collectivity. What comes from the collectivity is the government. Take the three functions of all power: to legislate, to judge, and to govern. (The latter is not execution, which is a hypocritical term from modern constitutional laws. The government does not execute the laws; the government governs. To declare war is not to execute a law but to govern. To present the budget is not to execute a law, except in the formal sense, which says that the government, every year, presents the budget. But what's in the budget? The law says nothing; the constitution says nothing. It's the government that decides, to the extent that it decides.) Thus, of the three functions, the collectivity among the Iroquois exercises two of them: it judges, probably; and it governs, i.e. it decides to make or not to make war with the neighbouring tribes. But it does not legislate. It does not institute.

Yet, for me, democracy – and here we rejoin the discussion, if you will, with Lefort – is not indeterminacy. It's explicit self-institution. It's the fact of saying, as the Athenians said, *edoxe tē boulē kai tō dēmō*, 'It seemed good to the counsel and to the assembly of the people'; or, as is said in certain modern constitutions, 'sovereignty belongs to the people.'[49] It's the people who are sovereign. Thus, the people can change the law (and in this respect it hardly matters if they don't change it, or if one subsequently adds that they exert it directly or by way of their representatives and that, after all, their representatives have everything cornered, and so on). It's this aspect that makes the difference, and I don't think there's a naturalness to democracy. Democracy is a very improbable regime, and a very fragile one, and that's precisely what shows that it's not natural.

Now, if it's okay with you, I will move on to the other question, 'What are the chances today, according to you, of getting the forms of direct democracy recognized, and what relationship can they maintain with the representative system?'

A. CAILLÉ: I would like to pose yet another question on the present point. After all, obviously, if I asked you that question it's because it matters to me. I think Baechler's thesis is more defensible than you're saying it is, but I believe it's necessary to come to an understanding on some things. A huge part of the total incommunicability on the issue, in this type of debate, is found in that you, like Lefort for that matter, fundamentally define democracy as a process of autonomy, as a process of collective self-questioning. And you say . . .

C. CASTORIADIS: And of self-institution.

A. CAILLÉ: And of self-institution. And you say (I was looking for a quotation from you and I did not find it) that, starting from the point when there is no explicit self-institution in ancient societies, there's no longer any question of talking about democracy. And you say more precisely that you don't intend to define democracy as a regime, as an institutional form. I think the whole debate lies here.

C. CASTORIADIS: That's not wholly accurate, but anyway.

A. CAILLÉ: I didn't find the quotation. Let's say that you're more attentive, like Lefort, to the movement of interrogation, of self-institution, and of collective self-creation than to the form of the political regime. Thus, you don't want to lead the discussion into this terrain about the form of the political regime. That can be understandable. But, as I see it, this nevertheless has some inconvenient features, which are by the way the same as those I signaled just before during your debate over the place of the West in relation to the universe. After all, as soon as you start reasoning in that way, setting apart the democratic, Helleno-Western, European historical moment, at bottom you're positing that all political regimes, roughly speaking, are equally valid. In any case you don't introduce criteria for distinguishing between them. Yet, it seems to me that, nevertheless, there's a considerable difference between the diverse, non-Western forms of power. We agree fully that they're not founded on collective self-interrogation, self-creation; but there is a considerable difference between powers founded on brute, physical violence or symbolic violence (which is not easy to define, but that's another matter) and a power founded on some form or another of consent and often even on a certain unanimity. This is the basis of Baechler's argument. You say that for you the natural tendency of humanity is the tendency to heteronomy, and you doubtless add political heteronomy...

C. CASTORIADIS: Total heteronomy. Why political?

A. CAILLÉ: Because we are speaking about politics at the moment. We're talking about democracy. That's why I say political heteronomy. After all, what you're saying is certainly true for the several recent millennia marked by the proliferation of forms of monarchy and empire. But Baechler's perspective consists in saying that this is, in the end, a relatively short historical period in light of the history of humanity. And he introduces with his reasoning a whole consideration of the primitive political regimes and the like. The question I'm asking you is this: Can one define democracy uniquely through an explicit, self-instituting dynamic, and can one dispense with asking the question of the foundation of the collective obedience and the foundation of the power? Can we dispense with distinguishing between regimes founded on violence, pure and simple, and regimes founded on a certain acceptance?

C. CASTORIADIS: Let's understand well: There's a difference between regimes founded on acceptance and regimes founded on violence pure and simple. By saying what I was saying before, I did not intend to say that when one adopts a political perspective everything is the same and everything is equally valid. Yet on this point – I will come back to the question of the regime – there's an entirely fundamental misunderstanding, and here again we meet up with the discussion with Lefort. What goes on in a consensual democracy – let's put that in quotation marks since nobody has gone there to see it up close, after all – of the type found among the Iroquois? Well, there is a consensus. But consensus as such, contrary to what is thought, contrary to what we seem to think today, has no value. There can wholly be a consensus in a society that's completely hierarchical. A good feudalism is a society based on consensus, and everybody is in their place. And that's still the society in Combray, according to Proust, where everybody was in their place and where a middle class woman who married a noble transgressed as much as the noble who married a prostitute. She was just as despicable because she married outside of her status, outside of her place. All of that, it was the European reality not all that long ago; but in feudalism it's the same thing. Now, doubtless, a regime established on consensus may appear to us as preferable. Effectively, it's more humane, even though.... There's a memorable text by Pierre Clastres on the initiatory rites in primitive societies in which one sees the extreme violence that gets paid for entry into that egalitarian society.⁵⁰

A. CAILLÉ: There were limits...

C. CASTORIADIS: It happened in the jungle with nests of ants on the skin and so on. Me, I would very much like for that to be more humane. But that's not directly our problem. Our problem is: Can we have a society that's truly free?

A. CAILLÉ: It's a society, in Clastres' sense, that's against domination. Nevertheless, there's a question...

C. CASTORIADIS: But where domination does exist, there's a heteronomy of a different type. And that's what Clastres failed to see; it was not his problem.

A. CAILLÉ: He says it. You just recalled it.

C. CASTORIADIS: No, he doesn't see the foundation of the heteronomy. The society is 'against the State'; but the society is in a certain sense for the transcendence of the source of its norms. And there, in the primitive societies he talks about, this transcendence is not a transcendence in the Western, metaphysical, Christian, Judeo-Christian sense or the like. It's the past of the societies; it's the word of the ancestors. And we have no power over that word.

I would like to mention a radical misunderstanding when you say that for me democracy is not a regime. It surprises me since obviously you have read the text called 'Done and To Be Done.'⁵¹ I think the source and perhaps the touchstone of all my divergences from Lefort are still found there. Things are entirely the contrary. Democracy is a regime. There's a description of the democratic regime that takes five pages at the end of that text. Democracy is a regime where there are rights, where there is *habeas corpus*, where there is direct democracy, and where the transformation of social and economic conditions permit the participation of citizens. I don't know whether it's necessary to agree about that. But I remind you that there's a description of the democratic regime, such as I have always thought of it and described it since *Socialisme ou Barbarie*, in the text called 'On the Content of Socialism.'[52] Why? Because it's absurd to speak of a regime, of a society, that self-institutes, if there aren't already instituted forms that allow for self-institution. Otherwise, it has no meaning. And for that reason the discourse of indeterminacy is, in my view, empty. For society to be able to be effectively free, to be autonomous, for it to be able to change its institutions, it needs institutions that allow it to do that. What, for example, does freedom, or the possibility for citizens to participate, or the fact of rising up against the anonymity of a mass form of democracy mean if there isn't, in the society we're talking about, something – which has disappeared in the contemporary discussions, including those of Lefort for that matter – which is *paideia*, the education of the citizen?[53] It's not about teaching them arithmetic; it's about teaching them to be a citizen. Nobody is born a citizen. How do they become one? By learning to be. They learn it, firstly, by watching the city in which they are found, and certainly not through this television they watch today. Yet, that counts as part of the regime. A regime of education is necessary. An economic regime is also necessary, for that matter. If a Berlusconi over there or a Bouygues over here owns the means for mass communication, we can ask what freedom of information there is and whether it hasn't been terribly reduced.[54] It isn't being jeopardized by the police but by infinitely more efficacious means. Take for instance the abrupt change that occurred in the Eastern countries as soon as the formal dictatorship was abolished. Before that, there was an interest in politics; now there isn't any more. Why? Because, only at this level of civic cretinization and practically at no other level did they westernize themselves straightaway. Immediately. In fifteen days. Three months after the fall of the Berlin Wall there were elections. The people who had fought against the regime got four-tenths of a percent of the vote. Those who had televisions from the West, and in particular Kohl and the Christian-Democrats, got the majority. Now there's a return of the pendulum, but it's for completely bad reasons, or almost.

Thus, democracy is for me a regime. I have just written, moreover, a text against Habermas and others called 'Democracy as Procedure and Democracy as Regime' where I say that democracy as procedure is meaningless because that procedure itself cannot exist as a democratic procedure if there are not institutional arrangements that allow for it as a regime.[55] And these institutional arrangements begin with the formation of the citizens and continue through the modalities that allow for inciting them to a maximal participation in the life that is political, collective, and so on. There's thus a radical misunderstanding here. And perhaps now you see better why Lefort, in his conception of indeterminacy, effectively refused to say anything about democracy as a regime. That's not the case with me.

A. CAILLÉ: Sure enough, I didn't find the quotation I thought I had read. I was mistaken. I confused you for a moment with Lefort. I offer you my apology. [*Laughter.*]

C. CASTORIADIS: Even if only visually, that would still be a bit much! [*Laughter.*] I think we're now cleared up on that point. I will come back to the line of your questions: 'What chance is there today according to you for getting forms of direct democracy recognized, and what relationship can they maintain with the representative system?'

In my view, there's no democracy except as direct. A representative democracy is not a democracy, and on this issue I agree not with Marx but with, among others, Rousseau: 'The English are free one day every five years, and so on.'[56] And not even one day every five years because by that day the die is cast. We're going to elect a president of the Republic next spring. What will freedom of the French be? It will be that of choosing between Balladur and Chirac, or Balladur and Delors.[57] That's all. The big argument against direct democracies in modern societies concerns the size of these societies. Yet the argument is made in bad faith, historically, concretely, and politically. Why historically? The representative regime as we practice it was unknown in antiquity. The ancients had magistrates; there were no representatives.[58] As far as I'm concerned, I'd like to have the magistrates. I would like to elect revocable magistrates and so on, but I don't want to be represented. I consider that to be an insult. The representative regime appeared in the medieval West. There was a very good book by the late Yves Barel, *La Ville médiévale*, that described the evolution of medieval society in this respect.[59] This regime appeared as of the eleventh or twelfth centuries in the cities that tended to self-govern. These cities counted perhaps three thousand or six thousand citizens, which makes up a tenth of the thirty thousand to forty thousand active citizens in Athens in the classical period, of which half undoubtedly assembled in the *ekklēsia*, and perhaps more when there were big decisions to make.[60] Yet they did not elect magistrates; they elected representatives. The idea of representation is thus a modern idea, and its rootedness in political heteronomy and political alienation is obvious. What are they, representatives? The term has become intransitive over time, but in the beginning it was transitive. The representatives are the representatives to and for the power. Thus, the fact of electing representatives presupposes that there's a king – and this is the classic case in England, for example – to and for whom one sends one's representatives. And the king governs. The 'King in his Parliament' is not an absolute monarch; it's the king in his parliament with the representatives of his subjects. This therefore has nothing to do with the size of the populace. And the proof of this is that one can ask the question from a different angle. In a modern nation, one says, there can't be direct democracy. Why can't there be direct democracy in a city of, say, one hundred thousand inhabitants, meaning fifty thousand active citizens? It's not the size that's to blame since in Athens this democracy was possible all while there were forty thousand active citizens. One could thus say: Let's establish direct democracy in units gathering forty thousand active citizens. But no, nobody raises the question from that angle. The argument from size is thus wholly sophistical and in bad faith.

I can't go into the critique of the representative regime here. It's been done a thousand times, and there's nothing new to add. The true argument for representative democracy, we mustn't forget, is that of Benjamin Constant in 'The Liberty of the Ancients Compared with that of the Moderns,' dating from about 1820, and already sketched out by Ferguson in *An Essay on the History of Civil Society*, in about 1770.[61] These people were not ideologues or theoreticians in bad faith; they were political people with their feet on the ground. What's the argument? It's that in modern societies what interests people is not the management of common affairs but the guarantee of their enjoyments. Those are Constant's terms, but Ferguson already said more or less the same thing. Constant adds that the majority of people in modern society – and this is an entirely Aristotelian argument – are occupied with the 'banausic' trades (which he would have said if he spoke Greek), i.e. mind-numbing trades, like with industry workers.[62] And as a result, it's entirely normal that there would be a censitary suffrage and that the only persons who vote are those who, through their way of life, have the leisure to reflect on public affairs and to occupy themselves with them.

What remains is the real question of direct democracy at the scale of modern societies, nations, perhaps continents, or even of the entirety of humanity. I don't have a response concerning the institutional forms that it could adorn. All I'm saying is that we will find, in the creations of the great political and social movements of the modern era, the germs of forms of regimes that allow for a direct democracy. For example, consider the form of the Paris Commune, or of the soviets (the true ones, before they were domesticated by the Bolsheviks), or of the workers' councils. Consider ones with an actually effective (as great as possible) power of the general assemblies, which means direct democracy for the ultimate decisions and, in a subsidiary way (as we would say now), a power for the delegates. But these delegates would obviously be elected and revocable at any instant and thus unable to expropriate the collectivity of its power. But, in all this, once again, I think that if there must be a democracy, it can only be direct. And it will not be able to be unleashed except from an enormous popular movement involving the great majority of the society. There's a creativity of society that, alone, is adequate to a problem of this type. If the society can't find forms for the exercise of power that are truly democratic, whether it be those I sketched or others that are perhaps more efficacious, then there will be nothing to be done, there will be, once again, a representative regime and, once again, what Marx called the backslide into all the 'old rubbish,' i.e. into the expropriation of power by the representatives, by the possessors, by the media people today, and the like. That's all for that question.

J. DEWITTE: In what was said just now, I recognize your positions, which I have known for a very long time. But I'm still surprised by what appears more and more to be their radicality. In the end you draw things up into a sharp alternative. You give an extreme form to the idea of autonomy, to the extent that if that's the case, then we arrive at no longer being able to recognize any institution or representation as having a value proper, even if only provisory. There is, on the one hand, a pure autonomy and, on the other hand, every form of institutionalization or representation. Yet those things do indeed make up a part of political history. All exteriority is, if that's the case, discredited.

I will take us back to a point a bit earlier in the discussion that had to do with the laws, with the example of the Iroquois. You had recounted your fundamental concept, your fundamental philosophical position, namely explicit self-institution. And I was saying to myself (well, it's perhaps trivial to say it, my apologies): But can we not conceive that one could freely recognize the laws as good? Must this idea of autonomy lead necessarily to a sort of compulsion to change? Here is where there risks being a slide between the exigency for freedom and autonomy, and something else perhaps. It seems to me that we need to look deeper into this aspect. You yourself recognize that there is no pure act of self-institution. You recognized just before that there is a limit to our power of action. So, this is also tied to our finitude. We inscribe ourselves in a tradition. We recognize that the world existed already before us. In that case, isn't there a possibility specifically that we may recognize certain laws as good without having the absolute need to change them, even if we do reserve for ourselves this possibility, if it's necessary?

C. CASTORIADIS: I'm afraid there's yet another misunderstanding. I take myself to be very bad, undoubtedly, at explicating my positions, since very often I do not recognize myself in the critiques that are made of me. Or else I'm blind about myself. I believe that I am, as much as one can be, autonomous in the domain of thought. I'm talking about myself, Castoriadis. What do I mean by that? I certainly do not mean that there is a compulsion for me to change and that every morning I get up, I take everything I have written, I flip through it, and I say to myself: I wrote that, so it can no longer be true, so it must be changed. No. Absolutely not. To be autonomous, for me, means that I continue to think; that I have new ideas from time to time; that I hope I continue to have them (unless Alzheimer's catches up to me); and that I give myself the right to say in writing (as it has occurred to me to do before) that what I wrote in such and such a place was false or insufficient and that it's necessary to look back over it and go further. And I have done that. You know my career. I started by being Marxist. Then, first, I rejected Marx's economics, then his theory of labour and technology, then his sociology, then his conception of history and his philosophy. And I set out to reinterpret the history of philosophy, to reject a lot of things that I had accepted and so on, and I continue to do that. And I could say the same thing with respect to Freud, for example, whom I respect enormously. I'm a psychoanalyst. But as for where I am now, there are very few things that are literally from Freud in what I think, in what I do, in what I say in the domain of psychoanalysis. It's like that. There's no compulsion to change. And I don't think of an autonomous society as dominated by a compulsion to change.

What is autonomy? It's when one may at each moment say: Is this law just? Heteronomy is when the question shall not be raised, as one says in the courts. The question will not be asked. It's forbidden. If you are a believing Jew, you cannot ask the question: Are the prescriptions of Exodus or Deuteronomy just or not? The question has no meaning. It has no meaning because the name of God is Justice and because these laws are the word of God. So, to say that it's unjust is to say that the circle is square. There you have it. This is the most extreme and most evolved, the most subtle and most grandiose formulation. But the same thing holds for all heteronomous societies. It's thus not a matter of daily putting the totality of the existing legislative arrangements onto the assembly's order of the day and of inviting the population to reapprove them or to change them. It's simply a matter of making room for the possibility – the effective possibility, of course – that the institutions can be altered without barricades, torrents of blood, havoc, and everything else being necessary for that.

Now, you say that all institutionalization is excluded. I say precisely the contrary. An autonomous society is a society that has institutions of autonomy, for example the magistrates. I said a while back that I accept these magistrates, and that not only do I accept them but I defend their necessity. It's only required that they be revocable. The whole question resides in this 'able' in revocable, and we see here to what (enormous) extent effective history surpasses all of our discussions. Because, of course, we have to write into the Constitution the clause, 'All magistrates are revocable by their mandators.' One would inscribe that into the democratic society as I conceive of it. But this clause in itself means nothing. First of all, it may be that the magistrates are irreproachable, or in any case excellent, and that therefore we let them accomplish their mandates and we re-elect them and so on. But it may also be that the people start to not give a damn and that therefore, as we have seen many times in strikes, student movements, and so on, the magistrates, the delegates, the representatives, the secretaries get entrenched. This is not necessarily because they want to get entrenched but because others say, 'Oh, there's Dewitte, there's Caillé, there's Latouche; they'll get us out of this mess. As for us, let's go to the movies!' Yet, what institutional measure do you want to enact against that? Of course, you can enact some institutional measures, as with certain ones that already exist. But we see what they lead to. It's certain that even if the magistrates get entrenched because the mandators don't exercise their right to revoke them, these magistrates cannot just do whatever they want. After all, there are courts, there's the Council of State, there's the Court of Audit, and so on. We see every day in the newspapers to what extent these means of control are weak. It's necessary to maintain such guardrails, of course; but they're not what's going to resolve the problem. The only solution is the activity of people. But we can't see in this activity a miracle that will either self-produce or not self-produce. The desire and the capacity of citizens to participate in political activities are themselves a political problem and a political task. And, in part, these things pertain to the institutions that induce them, that prescribe and create the citizens as carried towards that activity, and not towards the guarantee of their enjoyments. There you have it. That's what we must institutionalize.

A. CAILLÉ: [*To the audience.*] No more questions? . . . As for me, I'd like to return to a question. I'm sorry, but there are questions I've wanted to ask you for a long time. Since I have you at hand, I'll shamelessly take advantage. . . . Chantal?

CHANTAL MOUFFE: Yes, I'd like to return to this question. After all, I have a lot of sympathy for your positions. But it's really here that things get stuck. I would be disposed to accept, with you, that there cannot be any democracy except a direct one. Let's admit that. But immediately I'm going to say where the limitations are. I agree wholly that the argument from size is a bad faith argument. But I will, despite all of that, set out to defend what I would call the representative system, based in no way on arguments from size, nor in the least on arguments from Benjamin Constant. I believe that, at bottom, we have not yet truly elaborated the political philosophy that could justify this system – the representative regime – and that we would have to find an argument from another angle, which would have more to do with the defence of individual freedom. Let me explain. There's no democracy except a direct one, agreed. But does democracy guarantee individual freedom? In order to be able to guarantee it, isn't it rightly necessary to have, alongside the democratic institutions, other institutions that would have more to do with what I would call the question of pluralism? And thus, at bottom, this is why for me the best regime is always a mixed regime.

In your position, in Rousseau's position, there's likewise something that worries me. Doesn't it rest on the idea that, at bottom, the 'one' people, when they are going to decide directly within this representative democracy, are necessarily going to choose policies and make decisions that are going to guarantee the freedom of all? Isn't that basically the question raised by people like Stuart Mill? It's here, in what I call political liberalism, that there is, all the same, something important for thinking democracy today, namely the defence of minorities. After all, Switzerland is a much more democratic regime than lots of others, but that doesn't prevent it from making decisions that, regarding immigrants for example, are nevertheless very problematic. Doesn't your position in effect presuppose some kind of good unity which makes it such that, if we can decide entirely together, we are necessarily going to make good decisions? But I don't believe that. And that's why, alongside this democracy, institutions are necessary that aren't democratic – it's agreed that they aren't democratic – but which will rightly allow for guaranteeing, in certain conditions, individual freedom and a certain pluralism.

C. CASTORIADIS: I'm going to respond to this, but are there other questions?

A. CAILLÉ: A while back I was on the same trail as Chantal Mouffe. Personally, I'm wholly attached to this demand for direct democracy. It has totally disappeared from the French intellectual landscape for a long time now. We never hear it spoken of any more, except by you. I believe it's totally foundational. Yet I myself struggle with your formulation, since I don't think direct democracy can take the place of a regime of representative democracy. It seems to me that we have to reestablish it not in place of but as complementary to a representative democracy regime, more or less because of the reasons Chantal Mouffe just gave. Why is a representative democracy regime, which one may speak of as not democratic, nevertheless necessary? We can already see why, for de facto reasons. You alluded to the experiences of the soviets. They did not last very long, for reasons that need to be analysed and which are not a great mystery. What's the fundamental reason? What was direct democracy based on in the ancient era? It was based fundamentally on autochthony. It was based on the fact that the people had come from a like origin, from a like race, from a like culture, from a like soil, and on the fact that they shared common values, and that this made possible the unity of political decision. There's a problem faced by modern democracies, after the loss of a relative social homogeneity, which is also what Rousseau imagines, whose democracy is one of small producers. The question of modern democracies is simple. It arises right at the moment when there is no more autochthony, no more unity, no more economic, cultural, or social homogeneity, and when groups that are entirely different have to be put into relation. The question comes up at a meta-level, and it seems that it can't be solved any longer only through direct democracy. Another dimension is necessary, which could be the mixed regime. An appeal to something else is necessary. And you yourself said, moreover, that the institutions that create direct democracy are necessary. Of course. But that means this institution is not founded on direct democracy.

C. CASTORIADIS: First of all, direct democracy, the democratic regime I'm thinking of, is not a paradise on earth. It's not the perfect regime, and I don't know what perfect regime means. It's not a regime that is immunized, by design, against every error, aberration, folly, or crime. The Athenians committed them, and the French in 1793 as well. In North America it was a bit less extreme, but nevertheless. So this is not about that. But if we bring up this point, we must not forget that errors, aberrations, folly, and crimes were committed in overabundance by other regimes, including by representative regimes. The anti-red laws in the United States, for example, were voted in with all regularity by the House of Representatives and the Senate. I wrote a statement a few years ago that is perhaps, out of everything I've written, the thing I prefer the most: 'Nothing and nobody can protect humanity from its own madness.'[63] Democracy can't; and still less so can monarchy, since monarchy consists in the madness of the monarch, in Louis XV, in the cabal.

Now, the defence of individuals and of minorities? But I wholly agree. I will turn back once more to 'Done and To Be Done.'[64] We need reinforced arrangements, i.e. constitutional ones in the sense that their revision is subject, for example, to more restrictive conditions; to qualified majorities, if you will; to longer delays for reflection. These guarantee individual liberties, which we today call rights, and which comprise a *habeas corpus*, rules, e.g. like the one that ever since the Romans has said that there's no crime nor penalty without prior law. And all of this can and must be enhanced, since all of it is insufficient. One could just as well formulate arrangements defending minorities, different categories of minorities, and these arrangements could make up part of the Constitution. But are you proposing that we should have a Constitution that couldn't under any condition be revised? No, of course not. After all, the Constitution, even if it doesn't anticipate it, will be revised by the force of arms. We're at no less than the fifth French republican Constitution, not to mention the intermediate monarchical Constitutions. I don't know how many countries have had forty Constitutions, which have all become scraps of paper. The idea of a non-revisable Constitution is at once concretely and logically absurd. Just as you can't prevent the Swiss from using referendum to restrain the entry of migrants, you can never prevent the people, one day – and I'm going to say something deliberately ridiculous – from saying, 'All individuals of less than 1.6 meters or of more than 1.9 meters are deprived of the right to vote.' Since the other people are in the crushing majority, they could very well carry out that arrangement. What are you going to do? As for me, I would be against it. I would fight to the death against such an arrangement. I would try to rouse the people against it. If you admit a majority rule, you necessarily admit that, despite all guarantees, there's always the possibility that the people may go crazy and do this or that. Hitler was not brought to power by a majority but he might as well have been. Now, what should've been done about that? Deprive the Germans of the right to vote? That's what the movement of history is. We can fight against it, but we cannot guarantee ourselves against it through juridical arrangements. But what I absolutely do not see, and what seems to me to be truly a fallacy in your reasoning, and in Caillé's, is how the fact that the democracy would be representative, and not direct, constitutes a supplementary guarantee. We have right now in the United States a Congress that's preparing itself, if it dares, to do monstrosities.[65] I believe that what you are saying corresponds to an ideological tradition of the reinterpretation of Antiquity, which was one of the two between which the West has oscillated. This consisted in depicting the Athenian *dēmos* in its moments of folly – condemning the generals from Arginusae, or making some other such monstrous decision – all while forgetting all the other decisions that the same *dēmos* made over a hundred years, which culminated in a certain number of marvels with which we're all familiar.[66] The Athenian *dēmos* had moments of folly, but there were elected chambers of representatives that have had them equally and that made bad decisions. I don't see in what respect – and I implore you to reflect on this – a representative regime would guarantee individual liberties to a greater extent. It's not representatives who guarantee individual liberties; it's constitutional arrangements. And if the Constitution holds, if we then have the certainty that (for example, in the United States or in France) the restoration of slavery is impossible or – nothing is impossible – extremely improbable, then this is not because the Constitution says so. We would be cretins to think that. It's because we know that if there were a proposal for the restoration of slavery, a crushing majority of people would be ready to fight so that this restoration would not take place.

You, and Caillé too, associate me with Rousseau. Yet I have nothing to do with Rousseau on this issue. While it has often occurred to me to cite the sentence where Rousseau criticizes representative democracy, I absolutely do not agree with his conceptions about the general will, the banning of factions, and so on. I have nothing to do with all that. But I believe that there's nonetheless something in what you said that is very important and that is worth explicating. And here, there's a difference between modern democracy, between modern regimes, and the ancient regime. It's the conception of the representatives as representatives of particular interests. This aspect is effectively modern, and in a sense I'm against it. This would be a very long discussion, but I will reemploy an example that I like a lot. There was an arrangement in the Athenian laws, mentioned by Aristotle in the *Politics*, I believe, which said that whenever the assembly of the people had to decide to make or not make war against another bordering city, the citizens dwelling in the frontier regions didn't have the right to participate in the vote.[67] Why? Because they couldn't vote honestly, or else they'd be put into a 'double bind,' which leads to psychosis. Either they vote as citizens while forgetting the fact that their olive groves are going to be destroyed, their houses burned, and so on, and that's something harmful, or they vote as owners of houses, olive groves and so on, and they could care less about the interests of the city. Yet, it's this second case that gets actualized constantly in contemporary society. We say of the representatives that they're representatives of the people; but that's not the case. Look at what happens in reality; a little bit of concrete sociology is necessary, in the end. What are the American congresspeople? What are the French deputies? What do they defend above all? They defend the sectarian interests of their electors. The American Congress will say that it's necessary to support credits for Boeing because of Seattle, State of Washington; that it's necessary to support such and such base in Texas because it gives work to ten thousand people in the region, and so on. And here, we're talking about real people, but there are also more consistent interests. Behind the current representation there's the recognition of conflicting interests in society, and there's this idea that through representation, through this regime of indirect democracy, the interests can negotiate compromise solutions between themselves. What's the result? It's the current situation where, in effect, there are compromises, or 'give and take': 'Yes, agreed, you shall have such an augmentation of agricultural subsidies on the condition that you accept this.' And that's the total political powerlessness of the parliamentarians, i.e. the reason making it such that no decision is made, such that all the politicians talk about the necessary reforms and they never get them done.

Now, I agree with you in saying that we can't ignore the existence of particularities in society; that we can't speak in terms of unified society; that we must find a way so that these rights should be safeguarded as much as is reasonable. But it's necessary to maintain – and on this I am completely intransigent – the unity of the political body as a political body which has in view the general interest of society and not, for example, those of the winegrowers of the Midi. The winegrowers of the Midi are very respectable and they need to be protected, but we can't put them above the interests of the collectivity as a whole.

C. MOUFFE: Quickly. . . . I would like to clarify what I meant because I agree totally with your response. I do not at all want to defend the representative system such as it exists today, since it's certain that what's in play are particular interests. But I was thinking of a representative democracy to come. And thus what would this democratic regime to come, for which we want to struggle, rightly be? As for me, I believe it wouldn't rightly be a direct democracy regime but a representative democracy regime wherein the conflict would play out over the question, not of the conflict of interests, but of the conflict over the different interpretations of the common good. After all, I believe – and this is also what Alain said – that the big difference, in my view, between today's situation and the Greek situation is the question of homogeneity, the question of pluralism. And we can't take it as obvious – 'self-evident' as one says in English – that there is a single and like interpretation of the general interest that's more just than another. I agree entirely with you concerning the critique of the current society. But I believe that the society we want to struggle for would be a society in which the parties would rightly play a different role and would not be the representatives of particular interests. It's one in which the question would play out over the different interpretations of what the common good is. There's not just one single idea of the general interest, and it's rightly necessary to make room for conflict concerning these different interpretations. Thus, this would be a representative democracy that does not exist, of course.

A. CAILLÉ: A representative democracy that does not exist; a direct democracy that does not exist either.

C. CASTORIADIS: That's perfect. We're going in the right direction, since we're talking about what should exist and not the miserable current reality! But what we're calling the general interest, or the common good of the political body . . .

C. MOUFFE: It's not definable. It's a horizon.

C. CASTORIADIS: Certainly. It is not definable by a philosopher, by a Plato, nor by a Niklas Luhmann writing a theory of social systems, and even less so by a computer.[68] We're totally in agreement. But it is *open for discussion* by the citizens, and only the citizens can discuss it and then decide.[69] We thus have to ask ourselves: What are the questions that pertain to the general interest, and thus to political decision? And what are those that only concern, for example, the private sphere and aren't political in the strong sense of the term? Take homosexuality. In the United States, at least in certain states, it's considered as a crime, since the law is based on an arrangement that's found, I believe, in Leviticus.[70] But when Napoleon had to deal with homosexuality, he considered that it pertained to the private life of people and that politics didn't need to legislate on the matter. That's also my opinion, of course. Another example: Is the question of the equality of men and women a question of the general interest? For me, yes, incontestably. It's thus a political question. You may well repeat the words pluralism or cultural difference; but you'll have to establish the limits beyond which this pluralism is no longer valid. I'll reemploy once again a caricatured example (as that's a habit of mine and of my ancestor Socrates too), namely the right to kill those who don't please you. Is that a matter of cultural difference? Does the society in which we live admit as honourable the activity of headhunting, itself very honourable in certain tribes?

A VOICE: Among the Dayak people.

C. CASTORIADIS: Among the Dayak people, yes, notably. We say (and this is a political decision): No, this isn't a cultural difference; or: This is a cultural difference that isn't tolerable. In our society it's forbidden to kill. Now, as I already said jokingly, we can imagine a society rich enough to reserve a certain number of uninhabited islands of the Pacific for people who want to live as headhunters, or like in *The 120 Days of Sodom*.[71] Perfect. They freely go about killing themselves. . . .

A. CAILLÉ: You'll even furnish the victims?

C. CASTORIADIS: Yes, those who really want to be. Reread the preface by Paulhan to *Story of O*, with voluntary slavery and so on.[72] They'll be the ones to go live there. And if they lack victims, the butcherers will carry out massacres among themselves. But let's go back to what's essential, to the political decision. Contrary to what Plato thinks, there is no political *epistēmē*; that is a domain that pertains to *doxa*, to opinion. And, above all, democracy is such that all the *doxai* go head to head there freely, and only majority rule permits one to decide legitimately between them. We don't highlight this enough: The only foundation of majority rule is that in politics all the *doxai* are equivalent. And there's no procedural escape hatch of this type: Now discussion shall cease; we'll put all the opinions in a hat and we'll make a random draw. No. The number of opinions in favour of such a decision has a weight and creates a presumption of rectitude. But whether this majority would be acquired by referendum or by the vote of representatives, at this level I don't see the difference. The representatives will say, 'Headhunters aren't tolerated here.' And the majority of the people will say the same thing. I don't see how you can pull from that an argument for representative democracy, against direct democracy. Now, let's improve the devices for the protection of minorities. Of course. But it will surely be necessary to find a majority to define which minorities may legitimately make a claim for the said protection. And I hope we agree: Women are not a minority from this perspective; that problem comes up elsewhere. But time is getting on, and if we want . . .

A. CAILLÉ: We aren't forced to keep to the whole program!

DEBATE WITH THE *MAUSS* GROUP

C. CASTORIADIS: So, we're going to stop there? . . . That's quite alright, go ahead.

ANNE-MARIE FIXOT: You say that what's to be prioritized is the single, general interest and that it's open for discussion by the citizens. But the difficulty is that it's necessary to put the citizens into a position, or at least into a relation, for discussion. And that's what poses a problem for me today, since I realize that, as you said just before, many people lose interest in it and are indifferent. But it's also the case that certain people, given their socio-economic condition, can't manage to assume their place with regard to the general interest. What's to be done? How are we to think about this democracy to come? What's the role of information, of everyday education, not simply for children but equally for ourselves? And above all, what types of citizenship relations can we consider so as to succeed at having the general interest be taken into account effectively by the totality of the body of citizens and not simply by some people, even in the case of direct democracy?

C. CASTORIADIS: That's the fundamental problem. I am entirely in agreement with you. The participation of the citizens, at all levels of society, is not a matter in which it suffices to wait for a miracle. We must work at it intensively, introduce institutional arrangements that facilitate it. The central element, I repeat, is *paideia*, education; school is only a small part of it. Even Plato knew that, saying that 'the walls of the city educate the citizens.'[73] That's perfectly true, but so little put into practice. Now, when you evoke the socio-economic conditions, I fear that we would need to have another meeting, since we will never manage to finish today. It would be necessary to deal with the enormous problem of the economic and productive structure of society as well as the objective of economic activity.

A.-M. FIXOT: Lots of those who don't participate in political life say: We're in such a situation of exclusion; how could we even think about the general interest?

C. CASTORIADIS: Of course, there are exclusions. But there is also concrete apathy with many people. And even if certain of them were to have some interest in politics, they would not truly have the time to be occupied with it actively. The entire structure of society tends to prevent them from participating, and that stretches all the way from the structure of work to what one calls law. Ignorance of the law is no excuse. You were surely thinking of the amusing paradox that this adage so badly conceals. So, in court you're supposed to know everything and, at the same time, if your affair is the slightest bit complicated you will surely get a lawyer. That's someone who after four or five years of studies has specialized for still three or four more years in maritime law, in the law of this or that. That's an absurd situation, to which one can oppose the ancient system wherein all the laws were written on the marble, exposed. Everyone knew how to read and could get familiar with them. Our society is too complex for it to be able to be like that. But why should one have to submit to this complexity like a fate? What is important to us? Why should it be necessary to accept like a fate what historical evolution has given as, let's say, a spontaneous product, for example this capitalist society of the late twentieth century, with its enormous legislative complexity, which in the United States allows lawyers to earn more money than the industrialists they defend? And the aberrant modes of production, the walls covered with advertisements, and television such as it's imposed on us? Can we truly never call all of that into question? And why not invert things and say: We want a system of law such that every citizen can understand it and make do with it; we want an economic and productive system such that all the producers can participate in one way or the other in the management of

DEBATE WITH THE *MAUSS* GROUP

production. Do you see what I'm saying? What divine decree would impose upon us factories wherein fifty thousand workers, mind-numbed by their work, as Benjamin Constant said, would produce such types of products in such a way? A market economy that, in order to function well, requires a level of joblessness going up to 12–15 percent of the population? We can invert all of that and start by saying: We want a society in which all the citizens can participate in the common affairs. And in the face of that demand, there are practically no more indisputable givens. Our juridical system is contestable because it's anti-democratic; our system of production is contestable because it gets imposed by way of mind-numbing the workers for forty hours or more per week. Given these things, it's ridiculous to believe that there will be a Sunday full of political activity. It's necessary perhaps to invert the problem, to radicalize it, and to ask ourselves what society we really want.

S. LATOUCHE: It's clear that we have the response to your question of what society we want. By an immense majority, we want cars, washing machines, refrigerators, and so on. As president Bush said: The American standard of living is not negotiable.[74] Let nature die, but the American standard of living will remain as it is. And as a result we want the system to continue as it is; and at bottom we don't give a damn at all whether it's democratic or not. We don't completely not give a damn either, which means that we want, at once, to have our cake and eat it too. We want refrigerators, washing machines, automobiles, along with all that the system implies with respect to the dispossession of the citizen of political life by the techno-economic mega-machine. But may we not, despite everything, while remaining Aristotelian, recover the principle of the lesser evil? That's not the same as saying that this system would be managed by a totalitarian bureaucracy or that it would be managed by corrupt representatives in a Parliament such as it is. There is, nevertheless, a relative good.

C. CASTORIADIS: Obviously. Backed into a corner, if I'd had to choose between the extension of Soviet power such as it was in Europe and the maintenance of our rotten democracies, I would have been ready even to fight for the defence of these democracies. But I thought we were talking now about what the aim of politics should be. In May, there'll be a presidential election. I don't believe that I will vote. But if I should vote, it would not be for Balladur, for example.

A. CAILLÉ: For Chirac? [*Laughter.*]

C. CASTORIADIS: Neither. Nor for Arlette, for that matter![75] [*Laughter.*] But, in the end, I truly act in the relative here, like when I want to take the shortest route to go into the countryside.

S. LATOUCHE: Throughout this discussion there's an obstacle that Alain tried to raise at the start, but which we didn't reconsider subsequently in the debate and which we tend to forget. It's that we've been calling into question the entire economization of society and that, in fact, all of your reasoning presupposes that the economic imaginary has been completely decolonized.

C. CASTORIADIS: Do you have with you a copy of *Fait et à faire*?[76] Allow me, even if it is rather improper to cite oneself, to end this part of the discussion with a quotation:

> We thus arrive at the Gordian knot of the political question today. An autonomous society cannot be established except through the autonomous activity of the collectivity. Such an activity presupposes that people strongly invest in something other than the possibility of buying a new colour television. More profoundly, it presupposes that the passion for democracy and for freedom, for communal affairs, will take the place of distraction, cynicism, conformism, and the race to consume. In short, it presupposes, among other things, that the 'economic'

stops being the dominant or exclusive value. To respond to Ferenc Fehér, this is the 'price to be paid' for a transformation of society.

Let us put it even more clearly: The price to pay for freedom is the destruction of the economic as a central and, in fact, unique value. Is this too high a price? For me, certainly not. I infinitely prefer having a new friend over a new car. This is a subjective preference, of course. But 'objectively'? I willingly leave to the political philosophers the task of 'founding' (pseudo-) consumption as the supreme value. But there is something more important. If things continue on their present course, this price will have to be paid anyway. Who can believe that the destruction of the Earth will be able to continue at its present pace for another century? Who fails to see that it would accelerate further still if the poor countries were to industrialize? And what will the regime do when it cannot keep the populations in check by furnishing them constantly with new gadgets?[77]

I believe this text responds to your remark, or at least goes in the direction of your remark. I propose that we end here, since everyone has to be tired. As for me, in any case, I am.

J. DEWITTE: One little remark, nevertheless, that I wanted to make a while back. There's one of your writings that I've always appreciated, which is for me a very beautiful text, namely 'Development and Rationality,' which came out in *Esprit*, I believe.[78] Indeed, a very particular passage where you evoke the gesture of the Greek man who planted an olive tree . . .

C. CASTORIADIS: A cypress tree . . .

J. DEWITTE: I forgot that. Yes, because, moreover, in the olive tree there's something . . .

C. CASTORIADIS: Indeed, it was his daughter's dowry. When she turns twenty, they'll cut down this cypress tree in order to make the mast of a boat from it.

J. DEWITTE: What surprises me is that, in an encounter between Castoriadis and the *MAUSS* group, this aspect was not expanded upon. In this, after all, there's surely something like an economy that's otherwise than rational, that's a wager on the future, i.e. the foundation of a temporality that's not about immediate returns. Yet, that's exactly the way that I also understand the reflection that Alain rightly engaged in, the interpretation of the idea of the gift. It implies something like a transcendence, something that also goes beyond immediate interest. But then one gets into more of an ethical discussion or even metaphysical, which would be a different debate than this one, a debate to which I'm perhaps personally more amenable.

C. CASTORIADIS: We're engaging above all in a discussion about the ends of human life. But I agree entirely. I don't believe there can be politics without a certain position regarding the ends of human life. That takes us back to the question of pluralism. We're backed into a corner today. We can't continue to talk about indeterminacy or even simply the divergence of options. The ends of human life are realized by contemporary society in a certain form. The ends of human life, it's about the new television next year. That's it. Now, is this reality what we want? In any case, as Serge said, it's effectively what the majority wants at the moment.

S. LATOUCHE: The immense majority!

C. CASTORIADIS: The immense majority. Even those who aren't there are racing to get there: Eastern Europe, the under-developed countries. Yet this is incompatible with a true democracy, and it's even less and less compatible, in my view, with the truncated democracy we currently have.

Regarding what you're saying about the traditional Greek peasant, I'm completely in line with your view. After all, I myself cited at the beginning of our discussion that quasi-autarchic Greek village on the island of Tinos. Let's be clear: This allows us to express the core of the problem, but it wouldn't be a matter of a pure and simple return to the past. I'll take the liberty of directing you back, one last time, to another of my writings, reprinted in *Le Monde morcelé*, specifically 'Dead End?' (with a question mark).[79] Above all, it's about this autonomized race of techno-science with its industrialist and consumerist dimension, of course, but also with its purely scientific-technical aspect. We find more or less all of this in the interview with the doctor and biologist Jacques Testart in *Libération*.[80] He was asked: Do you think that, following the wishes of Madame Badinter, we'll one day make it possible for men to be pregnant, to bear a pregnancy?[81] He responded (after having resigned from those boards dealing with artificial insemination): 'I know there are labs in Chicago that are working in it. I can't tell you if it will be done or not; but I can tell you one thing: If it can be done, it will be done.'[82] There you have it. Contemporary techno-science. We don't ask ourselves whether we need something but only if we can do it. And if we can do it, then we do it. And subsequently we find a need, or we create one.

It's certain that we cannot continue in this fashion. But it's also certain that we can't purely and simply say we'll destroy everything and restart from zero. We are the first society in which the question of a self-limitation in the advancement of technologies and knowledges is proposed, not for religious or other reasons, nor political ones in the totalitarian sense (Stalin decreed that the theory of relativity is anti-proletarian), but for reasons of *phronēsis* in Aristotle's sense.[83] It's for reasons of prudence in the profound sense of the term. And I insist: I'm talking about the limitation not only of technology but also of science. What's essential in it, after all, is the notion of what's doable. And that's where that question becomes extremely difficult, including for me. After all, I would very much like an even more powerful Hubble to allow us to know if there were or weren't proto-galaxies fifteen billion years ago. That's a problem I'm passionate about. But the Hubbles and the satellites imply the totality of science and modern technology. Where are we going to lay down the limit, and who is going to lay it down, and on what grounds? Now that's a genuine question.

NOTES

1. This debate is preserved in reconstructed form in *La Revue du MAUSS semestrielle*, no. 2 (1993). —Trans.

2. Marcel Mauss's discovery of the gift, as explained by David Graeber, shows that 'almost everything we would call "economic" behavior was based on a pretense of pure generosity and a refusal to calculate exactly who had given what to whom. Such "gift economies" could on occasion become highly competitive, but [. . .] in exactly the opposite way from our own: Instead of vying to see who could accumulate the most, the winners were the ones who managed to give the most away. In some notorious cases, [. . .] this could lead to dramatic contests of liberality, where ambitious chiefs would try to outdo one another by distributing [huge amounts of goods] and even by destroying wealth – sinking famous heirlooms in the ocean, or setting huge piles of wealth on fire and daring their rivals to do the same. [. . .] In gift economies [. . .] exchange is about creating friendships, or working out rivalries, or obligations, and only incidentally about moving around valuable goods. As a result everything becomes personally charged, even property [. . .]. In a market economy it's exactly the other way around. Transactions are seen simply as ways of getting one's hands on useful things; the personal qualities of buyer and seller should ideally be completely irrelevant. As a consequence everything, even people, start being treated as if they were things too' (David Graeber, 'Give it Away,' *In These Times* 24, no. 19 (2000), retrieved 29

May 2019, https://inthesetimes.com/issue/24/19/graeber2419.html).—Trans.

3. See Claude Lefort, 'Réflexions sur le projet du MAUSS,' *La Revue du MAUSS semestrielle*, no. 2 (1993), 61–79.

4. Introducing the edition of *La Revue du MAUSS* containing Lefort's essay, Caillé had cautiously defended Lefort, stating that even though he does appear 'too discreet regarding the flaws of the era,' he nevertheless considers himself 'brutally critical of the "spirit of the times"' (Alain Caillé, 'Présentation,' *La Revue du MAUSS semestrielle*, no. 2 (1993), 9, n 8). —Trans.

5. Castoriadis appears to be paraphrasing Lefort, 'Réflexions.' —Trans.

6. Édouard Balladur (1929–present) was the conservative Prime Minister of France (1993–1995) who failed in a run for president in 1995. See also notes 57 and 75 below. —Trans.

7. Lefort conceives of modern democracy as establishing an indeterminacy (*indétermination*) at the centre of political power. This site, previously occupied by the nobility, becomes an 'empty place' subject to constant contestation. This shift involves 'a fundamental indeterminacy as to the basis of power, law and knowledge, and as to the basis of relations between *self* and *other*, at every level of social life' (Claude Lefort, *Democracy and Political Theory*, trans. David Macey (Cambridge: Polity Press, 1988), 17–19). Importantly, the French term *indétermination* has meanings not only corresponding to the English 'indetermination' and 'indefiniteness' but also to 'indecision,' a sense that seems also to concern Castoriadis here. He also seems to be responding to features of Lefort's contribution to *La Revue du MAUSS* which appear to play down *MAUSS*'s critique of the dominance of 'utilitarian' motives and 'techno-science' in modernity. See Lefort, 'Réflexions.' —Trans.

8. In several places Castoriadis ironically employs Orwell's already ironic expression. For example, see the debate with Daniel Cohn-Bendit: 'I think there's a singularity of the West or, as you'll prefer to say, of Greco-Western or European history, within universal history. I think this history creates something particular. As someone else might say: All cul-

tures are different, but there's one that's more different than the others. [*Laughter.*] More different just as much in its horror, for that matter, as in its characteristic that allows us to talk here tonight as we are talking' (Castoriadis, *De l'écologie*, 99–100). Castoriadis can allow himself this witticism because there would never be a possible misunderstanding among his listeners about what he means: 'I think that each culture, all cultures, have an equal, or better incomparable, value. I think, of course, that each collectivity, each nation, each people has to find its way. But I also believe that there exists in fact – something, for that matter, that's created by capitalism itself – a world society and a universal history in a sense that is no longer simply formal.'

9. The French *germe*, typically rendered as 'germ' by Castoriadis's translators, might be better rendered as 'seed,' so long as one remembers that the metaphor implies a germinated seed. The metaphorical use is common in French. See in particular Cornelius Castoriadis, 'The Greek *Polis* and the Creation of Democracy,' in *Philosophy, Politics, Autonomy: Essays in Political Philosophy*, ed. and trans. David. A. Curtis (New York: Oxford University Press, 1991), 84. —Trans.

10. For references to Herodotus on this point and Castoriadis's commentary, see Cornelius Castoriadis, *La Cité et les lois, Ce qui fait la Grèce, tome 2. Séminaires 1985–1986* (Paris: Éditions du Seuil, 2008), 252–54.

11. See the following note. —Trans.

12. In this section, the French term *la politique* will be translated as 'politics' and the term *le politique* will be translated as 'the political.' Castoriadis explains the significance of each term in what follows. —Trans.

13. The French term *homme* (man, person) is used frequently to refer to persons across genders. However, proof that the term's use in this way is contestable in French appears when both Castoriadis and Prat must clarify that they intend it neutrally (see pages 13 and 34, this volume). Hence, I have translated the term regularly as 'man,' 'men,' and so on. —Trans.

14. Castoriadis refers to ethnologist Pierre Clastres (1934–1977) who studied the indigenous tribes of Paraguay and the Venezuelan Amazon. See: Pierre Clastres, *Chronicle of the Guayaki Indians*, trans. Paul Auster (New York: Zone Books, 2000); *Society Against the State: Essays in Political Anthropology*, trans. Robert Hurley and Abe Stein (New York: Zone Books, 1989); and *Recherches d'anthropologie politique* (Paris: Éditions du Seuil, 1980).

15. Castoriadis is paraphrasing. See Lao-tzu, *Tao Te Ching*, trans. Steven Addis and Stanley Lombardo (Indianapolis: Hackett, 1993), especially sections 56–66, 72, 75–77. —Trans.

16. The text reads '*dans le royaume de Baïbar aux Indes*,' which appears to be an error of either transcription or reference. I read Castoriadis as trying to refer to the Mughal Empire (1526–1857) on the Indian subcontinent and its founder Babur (1483–1530). Thanks to Enrique Escobar for consultation on this issue. —Trans.

17. See 'Soudan, persécutions contre des chrétiens dans le sud du pays,' *Le Monde*, 9 December 1994.

18. See Castoriadis, *La Cité*, 216, 220, and 223.

19. See note 22 below on this terminology.—Trans.

20. See note 7 above. —Trans.

21. Castoriadis uses the term 'creation' (*création*) in a technical sense. It refers to something that emerges newly from nothing but which always emerges in and with social-historical or natural conditions on which it 'leans.' He contrasts creation with less radical concepts of the emergence of newness, such as production, deduction, difference, or mere epistemic unpredictability. See Cornelius Castoriadis, 'Time and Creation,' in *World in Fragments: Writings on Politics, Society, Psychoanalysis, and the Imagination*, ed. and trans. David A. Curtis (Stanford: Stanford University Press, 1997), 374–401, especially 395: 'As emergence of the otherness – of that which cannot be produced or deduced from what there is – being is creation: creation of itself, and creation of time as the time of otherness and of being.' See also Angelos Mouzakitis, 'Creation *ex nihilo*' and Jeff Klooger, '*Anlehnung* (Leaning On),' both in Suzi Adams, ed.,

Cornelius Castoriadis: Key Concepts (London: Bloomsbury, 2014), 53–64 and 127–34. —Trans.

22. The term 'radical imagination' refers to the *psychical* capacity to make 'a "first" representation arise out of a nothingness of representation'; it engages in 'positing, creating, bringing-into-being for the psyche/soma' (Castoriadis, *The Imaginary Institution of Society*, trans. Kathleen Blamey (Cambridge, MA: MIT Press, 1998), 283, 369). The term 'instituting imaginary,' by contrast, refers to *social-historical* creativity; it is the 'the fundamental "power" in society, the prime power on which all others depend' (Cornelius Castoriadis, 'Power, Politics, Autonomy,' in *Philosophy, Politics, Autonomy: Essays in Political Philosophy*, ed. and trans. David. A. Curtis (New York: Oxford University Press, 1991), 167–68). Castoriadis sometimes refers to the latter power as the 'anonymous collective,' a term emphasizing that social meaning belongs to no one and yet is a precondition for individual meaning. See Cornelius Castoriadis, *The Imaginary Institution of Society*, trans. Kathleen Blamey (Cambridge, MA: MIT Press, 1998), 111–12. —Trans.

23. Castoriadis distinguishes between the creativity found in all societies, on the one hand, and the institutionally-supported possibility of reflective evaluations of social creations (as possibly either 'good' or 'bad') from the standpoint of autonomy, on the other hand. See, for example, Castoriadis, 'Power,' 172: 'We must not forget, indeed, that the instituting imaginary *as such* as well as its works are neither "good" nor "bad" – or rather that, from the reflective point of view, they can be either the one or the other to the most extreme degree (the same being true of the imagination of the singular human being and its works). It is therefore necessary to shape institutions that make this collective reflectiveness effectively possible as well as to supply it with the adequate instruments.' —Trans.

24. Castoriadis paraphrases Maximilien Robespierre, *Oeuvres complètes de Maximilien Robespierre, 10 volumes* (Paris: Société des études Robespierristes, 1950–67), VIII, 81. —Trans.

25. See Cornelius Castoriadis, 'Le Délabrement de l'Occident,' in *La Montée de l'insignifiance, Les Carrefours du labyrinth IV* (Paris: Édi-

tions du Seuil, 1996), 61–63; and 'La Montée de l'insignifiance,' in *La Montée*, 97–99.

26. In this sentence and in the following paragraph, Latouche's use of the French pronoun *on* ('we') may also be translated as 'they' or 'one,' hence making this sentence less of a self-condemnation. That said, Latouche does employ the term *nos*, which means 'our,' in the same context (in the second-to-last sentence of the next paragraph). For this reason, I have retained the casual translation of *on* as 'we' throughout this segment. —Trans.

27. René Descartes suggests that we might be able to 'render ourselves, as it were, masters and possessors of nature' (René Descartes, *Discourse on Method: Third Edition*, trans. Donald A. Cress (Indianapolis: Hackett, 1998), 35). —Trans.

28. Latouche's paraphrase may refer to Francis Bacon's comment that 'the secrets of nature reveal themselves better through harassments applied by the arts than when they go on in their own way' (Francis Bacon, *The New Organon* (Cambridge: Cambridge University Press, 2000), 81). —Trans.

29. The term *agora*, in addition to referring to the open site of the markets and public gatherings (of various kinds) in historical Athens especially, also serves more generally in Castoriadis's work as the concept of the socially instituted zone of public/private mixture. He distinguishes it, on the one hand, from the public/public zone of the *ekklēsia* (or assembly), which referred to the official space for the popular assembly of all citizen-lawmakers. On the other hand, he also distinguishes it from the private/private zone of the *oikos*, which in Greek refers to the family or household. See 'Done and To Be Done,' in *The Castoriadis Reader*, trans. and ed. David A. Curtis (Oxford: Blackwell, 1997), 405–10; and 'Democracy as Procedure and Democracy as Regime,' trans. David A. Curtis, *Constellations* 4, no. 1 (April 1997), 7. —Trans.

30. Castoriadis frequently describes modernity as beholden to a social imaginary signification conflicting with the project of autonomy, namely the project of 'rational mastery' (*maîtrise rationelle*). It consists in the projection and promotion of endless expansion of rational control over

society and nature. See Karl E. Smith, 'Modernity,' in Adams, *Cornelius*, 179–90. —Trans.

31. 'When God calculates and exercises his thought, the world is made' (G.W. Leibniz, 'Dialogue (1677),' in *Philosophical Essays*, trans. Roger Ariew and Daniel Garber (Indianapolis: Hackett, 1989), 270, note 323). —Trans.

32. Charles Baudelaire, *The Intimate Journals of Charles Baudelaire*, trans. Christopher Isherwood (New York: Marcel Rood Co., 1947), XCIX. —Trans.

33. For *MAUSS*, 'primary sociality' refers to the relationships that structure 'alliance and parenthood, camaraderie and friendship, associative life.' This is where 'relationships from person to person take place,' and these 'always function according to the obligation to give, to receive and to return.' These are contrasted with 'secondary sociality,' e.g. superstructural relations such as 'market and state' (Alain Caillé, 'Utilitarianism and Anti-Utilitarianism,' *Thesis Eleven* 33, no. 1 (August 1992), 67). —Trans.

34. See Alexis de Tocqueville, *The Ancien Régime and the French Revolution*, trans. Arthur Goldhammer (Cambridge: Cambridge University Press, 2011). For Lefort's reading of Tocqueville, see Lefort, *Democracy* and Lefort, 'Réflexions,' 71–75. —Trans.

35. Castoriadis emigrated from Greece to Paris in 1945. See François Dosse, *Castoriadis : Une vie* (Paris: La Découverte, 2014). —Trans.

36. See Aristotle, *Nicomachean Ethics*, 1161b. —Trans.

37. See Aristotle, *Politics*, 1254b. —Trans.

38. See Thucydides, *History of the Peloponnesian War*, 5.7.85–112.

39. See Castoriadis, *La Cité*, 39 and note 29.

40. On this theme, see Saint Paul, *I Corinthians*, 12:13; *Colossians* 3:11; *Galatians*, 3:28 (paraphrased above) and 4:7. See also the commentary in Cornelius Castoriadis, *Sujet et verité dans le monde social-historique, Séminaires 1986–1987. La création humaine I* (Paris: Éditions du Seuil, 2002), 353 (and the note on page 469).

41. Castoriadis paraphrases Bartolomé de las Casas (1484–1566), the first Spanish colonist to serve as 'Protector of the Indians.' —Trans.

42. Castoriadis refers to the Peasants' Revolt in England in 1381. —Trans.

43. The following exchange between L. Baslé and C. Castoriadis was not retained for the earlier publication in *La Revue du MAUSS*.

44. See Jean Baechler, *Précis de la démocratie* (Paris: Calmann-Lévy, 1994). See also Jean Baechler, *La Grande Parenthèse (1914–1991), Essai sur un accident de l'histoire* (Paris: Calmann-Lévy, 1993).

45. 'The *privatization* of individuals is the most striking trait of modern capitalist societies' (Cornelius Castoriadis, 'Modern Capitalism and Revolution,' in *Political and Social Writings, Volume 2: 1955–1960*, ed. and trans. David A. Curtis (Minneapolis: University of Minnesota Press, 1988), 238). —Trans.

46. See Jean Baechler, *Démocraties* (Paris: Calmann-Lévy, 1985), where Baechler, who devoted 728 well-documented pages to laying out his thesis, writes: 'Because of the venerable but erroneous university distinctions, to pursue historical studies is to occupy oneself almost exclusively with kingdoms and empires. Democracies then figure in as improbable exceptions – Greece, medieval cities, contemporary Western nations – and one has thus laid out the exhaustive list. This conviction touches on the truth insofar as one envisions the human adventure across only approximately five thousand years. But if one purports to grasp it across the whole species from the beginning, across thirty-five or forty thousand years, across the whole planet, then one is driven into a Copernican reversal. A massive empirical given imposes itself: democracy is, it seems, the normal condition of humanity; it is the kingdoms and empires that make up the exception and that stand in need of being explained. As always, the most important propositions, those which require years of intellectual wandering before imposing themselves, appear once enunciated to be obvious. After all, all it took was to draw the ultimate consequences of the conceptual analysis to conclude that *the human is naturally democratic* and that *democracy is the natural regime of the species* Homo sapiens' (italics in original). —Note by Alain Caillé

47. See, for example, Friedrich August von Hayek, *The Road to Serfdom* (London: Routledge Press, 1944). —Trans.

48. See note 14 above on the work of Clastres.

49. The Greek phrase noted here prefaced the decrees passed by the Athenian general assembly of citizens (*ekklēsia*), when those laws had been passed to them from the *boulē*, i.e. the council of five hundred allotted volunteer citizens. When a decree originated in the general assembly itself, it was passed with only *edoxe tō dēmō* ('It seemed good to the [assembly of the] people'). See Mogens H. Hansen, *The Athenian Democracy in the Age of Demosthenes: Structure, Principles, and Ideology*, trans. J.A. Crook (Norman: University of Oklahoma Press, 1999), 125–40. —Trans.

50. See Pierre Clastres, 'Of Torture in Primitive Societies,' in *Society*, 177–88.

51. Castoriadis, 'Done.'

52. Cornelius Castoriadis, 'On the Content of Socialism, I–III,' in *Political and Social Writings, Volume 2: 1946–1955*, ed. and trans. David A. Curtis (Minneapolis: University of Minnesota Press, 1988), 290–333; and *Political and Social Writings, Volume 2: 1955–1960*, ed. and trans. David A. Curtis (Minneapolis: University of Minnesota Press, 1988), 90–192.

53. The Greek term *paideia* refers broadly to education, especially as focused on making one fit for life in the *polis*. In Castoriadis's usage, as Straume clarifies, the term has, on the one hand, a descriptive use referring to the function in all societies whereby persons come to sublimate the norms of their society, i.e. become socialized. On the other hand, Castoriadis uses the term – often qualified as *paideia* in the 'true' or 'profound' sense – to speak of a specific *type* of socialization or sublimation, only found in some societies, which helps persons become invested in autonomous practices (e.g. investments in truth-seeking, in self-governance, in sustaining the material supports required to reproduce those investments in future generations, and so on). See Ingerid S. Straume, '*Paideia*,' in Suzi Adams, ed., *Cornelius Castoriadis: Key Concepts* (London: Bloomsbury, 2014), 143–53. See also Stathis Gourgouris, 'Philosophy and Sublimation,' *Thesis Eleven* 49, no. 1 (1997), 31–43. —Trans.

54. Silvio Berlusconi (1936–present) established a media empire before becoming prime minister of Italy several times (first in 1994). Francis Bouygues (1922–1993), followed by son Martin (1952–present), founded the French company Bouygues, a company with wings in construction, telecommunication, and media. —Trans.

55. The French term *disposition* will be consistently translated as 'arrangement.' In a spatial sense, it might translate as 'layout,' 'placement,' or 'positioning.' In contexts of human action broadly, it may translate as 'tendency,' 'propensity,' 'readiness,' or 'character'; and Castoriadis likely sometimes uses it as a translation of Aristotle's *hexis*, which has also been translated as 'habit,' 'state,' or 'constitution' (e.g. of a person). In specific contexts referring to laws or constitutions, it might translate better as 'provision,' 'stipulation,' or even 'clause.' Furthermore, readers should bear in mind the proximity between the terms *disposition* and *dispositif* (usually translated as 'device' or 'apparatus'). For a genealogy of this term, see Giorgio Agamben, 'What is an Apparatus?' in *What is an Apparatus? and Other Essays* (Stanford: Stanford University Press, 2009), 14: 'Further expanding the already large class of Foucauldian apparatuses, I shall call an apparatus literally anything that has in some way the capacity to capture, orient, determine, intercept, model, control, or secure the gestures, behaviors, opinions, or discourses of living beings.' —Trans.

56. See Jean-Jacques Rousseau, *Of the Social Contract*, in *The Social Contract and Other Later Political Writings*, trans. Victor Gourevich (Cambridge: Cambridge University Press, 1997), Book III, Chapter 15. See the commentary in Castoriadis, *La Cité*, 27.

57. Jacques Delors (1925–present) was a French socialist politician who would decide not to run for president in 1995. Jacques Chirac (1932–present) would eventually win the election via runoff and remain president from 1995–2007. He had already served, among other roles, as Prime Minister of France (1974–1976; 1986–1988). See also note 75. —Trans.

58. The term 'magistrates' (Greek: *archai*) in the ancient context refers to 'officials appointed by election or sortition for a shorter period, mostly a year, and entrusted with the day-to-day administration of the

polis and the carrying into effect of the decisions made by the Assembly, the Council and the courts' (Mogens H. Hansen, *Polis: An Introduction to the Ancient Greek City-State*, trans. J.A. Crook (Oxford: Oxford University Press, 2006), 171, n 58). Elsewhere, Castoriadis clarifies that generally 'magistrates were being appointed by drawing lots or by rotation. [. . .] Everyone is capable of governing, so lots are drawn. Why? Because politics is not the business of specialists. [. . .] [For] specialized activities – the setting up of shipyards, the construction of temples, the waging of war – specialists are necessary. Therefore, such specialists are elected. That's what an election is because election means election of the best. And what is the election of the best based on? Well, that's where the education of the people comes in, since they are led to choose' (Cornelius Castoriadis, 'No God, No Caesar, No Tribune!' trans. Gabriel Rockhill et alii, in *Postscript on Insignificance: Dialogues with Cornelius Castoriadis*, trans. Gabriel Rockhill and John V. Garner (New York: Continuum, 2011), 11–12). —Trans.

59. See Yves Barel, *La Ville médiévale. Système social, système urbain* (Grenoble: Presses universitaires de Grenoble, 1977).

60. See note 29 above on the *agora*, *ekklēsia*, and *oikos*.—Trans.

61. See Adam Ferguson, *An Essay on the History of Civil Society* (Cambridge: Cambridge University Press, 1996); and Benjamin Constant, 'The Liberty of the Ancients Compared with that of the Moderns,' in *Political Writings*, trans. (Cambridge: Cambridge University Press, 1988). See also the commentary in Castoriadis, *La Cité*, 32–33, 149–53, and 218–19.

62. The term 'banausic' stems from the Greek *banausikos*, meaning 'of or for artisans.' —Trans.

63. 'Nobody can protect humanity from folly or suicide' (Cornelius Castoriadis, 'The Greek *Polis* and the Creation of Democracy,' in *Philosophy, Politics, Autonomy: Essays in Political Philosophy*, ed. and trans. David A. Curtis (Oxford: Oxford University Press, 1991), 115).

64. See Castoriadis, 'Done,' 405–13; see also Castoriadis, 'Democracy.' —Trans.

65. This surely refers to the efforts of the Republican majority in Congress to impose a strictly balanced budget on the Clinton administration in 1994–1995, with an important reduction in social aid and medical coverage for the most destitute.

66. See Castoriadis, *La Cité*, 204 and 207–8.

67. See Aristotle, *Politics*, 1330a20.

68. Regarding the German sociologist Niklas Luhmann (1927–1998), see, above all, in French, *Politique et complexité. Les contributions de la théorie générale des systèmes* (Paris: Éditions du Cerf, 1999).

69. The French term translated as 'open for discussion' is *discutable*, which might also be rendered as 'discussable' or simply 'discutable.' —Trans.

70. See *Leviticus* 20:13: 'If a man lies with a male as with a woman, both of them have committed an abomination; they shall be put to death; their blood is upon them' (NSRV).

71. See Marquis de Sade, *The 120 Days of Sodom*, trans. Will McMorran and Thomas Wynn (London: Penguin Books, 2016). —Trans.

72. See Jean Paulhan, 'Preface,' in Pauline Réage, *Story of O*, trans. Sabine D'Estrée (New York: Grove Press, 1966), xxi–xxxvi. —Trans.

73. Castoriadis may be referring to the words of the Athenian in Plato's *Laws*: 'A wall never contributes anything to a town's health, and in any case is apt to encourage a certain softness in the souls of the inhabitants. It invites them to take refuge behind it instead of tackling the enemy and ensuring their own safety by mounting guard night and day; it tempts them to suppose that a foolproof way of protecting themselves is to barricade themselves in behind their walls and gates, and then drop off to sleep, as if they were brought into this world for a life of luxury. It never occurs to them that comfort is really to be won by the sweat of the brow, whereas the only result of such disgusting luxury and idleness is a fresh round of troubles, in my view' (Plato, *Laws*, trans. Trevor J. Saunders, in Plato, *Complete Works*, ed. John M. Cooper (Indianapolis: Hackett, 1997), 778e–779a). —Trans.

74. George H.W. Bush, father of George W. Bush. [The former said in 1992, 'The American way of life is not negotiable.' —Trans.]

75. Arlette Laguiller (1940–present) was a candidate multiple times for the French presidency (1974–2007) with the Trotskyist tendency *Lutte Ouvrière*. It was predictable by 1994 that she would gain only a small percentage of the vote each time. Thus, part of the humour here arises from the fact that Castoriadis has eliminated the competitive right (i.e. Chirac and Balladur) and the non-competitive left (Laguiller). He thus silently passes over the obvious remaining option of the competitive left, i.e. *Parti Socialiste*. Castoriadis would comment in 1997 that many people voted for the eventual *Parti Socialiste* candidate Lionel Jospin in 1995 (who won the first round, only to lose the second round to Chirac) because they 'were sickened by fourteen years of pretended socialism in which the principal exploit was to introduce into France the most unbridled liberalism and to start to dismantle what there had been in the way of social conquests in the preceding period' (Cornelius Castoriadis, 'De l'Autonomie en politique. L'Individu privatisé,' recorded by Robert Redeker, *Le Monde diplomatique*, February 1998, 23). —Trans.

76. Castoriadis refers to the volume *Fait et à faire*, cited above, and specifically to the essay of the same title, 'Done and To Be Done,' also cited above. —Trans.

77. Castoriadis, 'Done,' 416 (translation modified).

78. See Cornelius Castoriadis, 'Reflections on "Rationality" and "Development",' in *Philosophy*, 175–218.

79. See Cornelius Castoriadis, 'Dead End?' in *Philosophy*, 243–75.

80. Jacques Testart (1939–present) is a French biologist who helped establish *in vitro* fertilization in France. —Trans.

81. Élisabeth Badinter (1944–present) is a French feminist author who had discussed this prospect in her writings. —Trans.

82. This anecdote is unconfirmed and likely a paraphrase. For a list of Testart's academic and popular press publications, see 'Jacques Testart, critique de science,' accessed 25 May 2019, http://jacques.testart.free.fr/. See also Élisabeth Badinter, 'Ces hommes qui veulent enfanter,' *Le Nouvel Observateur*, no. 1121, 2–8 May 1986. See also the parallel discussion in Castoriadis, 'Dead End?' 249–50. —Trans.

83. The Greek term *phronēsis* is usually translated today as 'practical wisdom' or 'practical reason,' or, classically, as 'prudence.' See especially Aristotle, *Nicomachean Ethics*, Book VI. —Trans.

REFERENCES

Adams, Suzi, ed. *Castoriadis and Ricoeur in Discussion: On Human Creation, Historical Novelty, and the Social Imaginary*. Lanham, MD: Rowman & Littlefield, 2017.
Adams, Suzi. *Castoriadis's Ontology: Being and Creation*. New York: Fordham University Press, 2011.
Adams, Suzi, ed. *Cornelius Castoriadis: Key Concepts*. London: Bloomsbury, 2014.
Adams, Suzi. 'Castoriadis and Ricoeur on the Hermeneutic Spiral and the Meaning of History: Creation, Interpretation, Critique.' In *Castoriadis and Ricoeur in Discussion: On Human Creation, Historical Novelty, and the Social Imaginary*, edited by Suzi Adams, 111–38. Lanham, MD: Rowman & Littlefield, 2017.
Agamben, Giorgio. 'What is an Apparatus?' In *What is an Apparatus? And Other Essays* Stanford, CA: Stanford University Press, 2009.
Arendt, Hannah. *Between Past and Future: Six Exercises in Political Thought*. New York: Viking Press, 1961.
Arendt, Hannah. 'What is Freedom?' In *Between Past and Future: Six Exercises in Political Thought*, 143–71. New York: Viking Press, 1961.
Arnason, Johann P. 'Castoriadis and Ricoeur on Meaning and History: Contrasts and Convergences.' In *Castoriadis and Ricoeur in Discussion: On Human Creation, Historical Novelty, and the Social Imaginary*, edited by Suzi Adams, 49–76. Lanham, MD: Rowman & Littlefield, 2017.
Aron, Raymond. 'Le Paradoxe du même et de l'autre.' In *Échanges et communications: Mélanges offerts à Claude Lévi-Strauss, à l'occasion de son 60ème anniversaire (Tomes I et II)*, edited by Jean Pouillon et Pierre Maranda. The Hague: Mouton, 1970.
Bachofen, Blaise, Sion Elbaz, and Nicolas Poirier, eds. *Cornelius Castoriadis. Réinventer l'autonomie*. Paris: Éditions du Sandre, 2008.
Bacon, Francis. *The New Organon*, edited by Lisa Jardine and Michael Silverthorne. Cambridge: Cambridge University Press, 2000.

Badinter, Élisabeth. 'Ces hommes qui veulent enfanter.' *Le Nouvel Observateur*, no. 1121, 2–8 May 1986.
Baechler, Jean. *Démocraties*. Paris: Calmann-Lévy, 1985.
Baechler, Jean. *La Grande Parenthèse (1914–1991), Essai sur un accident de l'histoire*. Paris: Calmann-Lévy, 1993.
Baechler, Jean. *Précis de la démocratie*. Paris: Calmann-Lévy, 1994.
Barel, Yves. *La Ville médiévale. Système social, système urbain*. Grenoble: Presses universitaires de Grenoble, 1977.
Baudelaire, Charles. *The Intimate Journals of Charles Baudelaire*, translated by Christopher Isherwood. New York: Marcel Rood Co., 1947.
Beauvoir, Simone de. *Ethics of Ambiguity*, translated by Bernard Frechtman. New York: Citadel, 1976.
Bernal, Martin. *Black Athena: The Afroasiatic Roots of Classical Civilization, v. 1, The Fabrication of Ancient Greece 1785–1985*. New Brunswick: Rutgers University Press, 1987.
Boilleau, Jean-Luc. *Conflit et lien social, la rivalité contra la domination*. Paris: La Découverte, 1992.
Boilleau, Jean-Luc, ed., *De la fin de l'histoire*. Paris: Éditions du Félin, 1992.
Bourdieu, Pierre. 'Intellectual Field and Creative Project.' *Social Science Information* 8, no. 2 (1969): 89–119.
Caillé, Alain. *Critique de la raison utilitaire : un manifeste anti-utilitariste*. Paris: La Découverte, 1989.
Caillé, Alain. 'Éditorial : La Non-utilité des femmes.' *Bulletin du MAUSS*, no. 10 (1984): 3–9.
Caillé, Alain. 'De Marx à Mauss sans passer par Maurras.' In *Marx après les marxismes, tome 1: Marx à la question*, edited by Michel Vakaloulis and Jean-Marie Vincent, 105–26. Paris: L'Harmattan, 1997.
Caillé, Alain. 'Présentation.' *La Revue du MAUSS semestrielle*, no. 2 (1993): 5–10.
Caillé, Alain. 'Présentation : Développement, éthique et politique.' *Bulletin du MAUSS*, no. 24 (December 1987): 3–9.
Caillé, Alain, ed. *La Revue du MAUSS semestrielle*, no. 2 (1993).
Caillé, Alain, ed. *La Revue du MAUSS semestrielle*, no. 13 (1999).
Caillé, Alain, ed. *La Revue du MAUSS semestrielle*, no. 14 (1999).
Caillé, Alain. 'Utilitarianism and Anti-Utilitarianism.' *Thesis Eleven* 33, no. 1 (August 1992): 57–68.
Caillé, Alain and Sylvain Dzimira. 'De Marx à Mauss, sans passer par de Maistre ni Maurras.' *La Revue du MAUSS semestrielle*, no. 34 (2009): 65–95.
Castoriadis, Cornelius. 'Breaking the Closure: Cornelius Castoriadis in Dialogue with Robert Legros.' In *Postscript on Insignificance: Dialogues with Cornelius Castoriadis*, translated by Gabriel Rockhill and John V. Garner, 93–107. New York: Continuum, 2011.
Castoriadis, Cornelius. *The Castoriadis Reader*, edited and translated by David A. Curtis. Oxford: Blackwell, 1997.
Castoriadis, Cornelius. *La Cité et les lois, Ce qui fait la Grèce, tome 2. Séminaires 1983–1984*. Paris: Éditions du Seuil, 2008.

REFERENCES

Castoriadis, Cornelius. 'Contribution de Cornelius Castoriadis (philosophe, EHESS).' *Politix* 1, no. 1 (Winter 1988): 16–18.

Castoriadis, Cornelius. *D'Homère à Héraclite, Ce qui fait la Grèce, tome 1. Séminaires 1982–1983*. Paris: Éditions du Seuil, 2004.

Castoriadis, Cornelius. 'Le Délabrement de l'Occident.' In *La Montée de l'insignifiance, Les Carrefours du labyrinth IV*, 58–81. Paris: Éditions du Seuil, 1996.

Castoriadis, Cornelius. 'De l'Autonomie en politique. L'Individu privatisé,' recorded by Robert Redeker. *Le Monde diplomatique*, February 1998, 23.

Castoriadis, Cornelius and Daniel Cohn-Bendit. *De l'écologie à l'autonomie*. Paris: Éditions du Seuil, 1981.

Castoriadis, Cornelius. *Democracia y relativismo*. Madrid: Trotta, 2007.

Castoriadis, Cornelius. 'Democracy as Procedure and Democracy as Regime,' translated by David A. Curtis. *Constellations* 4, no. 1 (April 1997): 1–18.

Castoriadis, Cornelius. *Démocratie et relativisme. Débat avec le MAUSS*, edited by Enrique Escobar, Myrto Gordican, and Pascal Vernay. Paris: Mille et Une Nuits, 2010.

Castoriadis, Cornelius. *Devant la guerre*. Paris: Fayard, 1981.

Castoriadis, Cornelius. *Domaines de l'homme, Les Carrefours du labyrinth II*. Paris: Éditions du Seuil, 1986.

Castoriadis, Cornelius. 'Done and To Be Done.' In *The Castoriadis Reader*, edited and translated by David A. Curtis, 361–417. Oxford: Blackwell, 1997.

Castoriadis, Cornelius. *Fait et à faire, Les Carrefours du labyrinth V*. Paris: Éditions du Seuil, 1997.

Castoriadis, Cornelius. 'The Greek and the Modern Political Imaginary.' In *World in Fragments: Writings on Politics, Society, Psychoanalysis, and the Imagination*, edited and translated by David A. Curtis, 84–107. Stanford: Stanford University Press, 1997.

Castoriadis, Cornelius. 'The Greek *Polis* and the Creation of Democracy.' In *Philosophy, Politics, Autonomy: Essays in Political Philosophy*, edited and translated by David. A. Curtis, 81–123. New York: Oxford University Press, 1991.

Castoriadis, Cornelius. *Histoire et création, Textes philosophiques inédits (1945–1967)*. Paris: Éditions du Seuil, 2009.

Castoriadis, Cornelius. *The Imaginary Institution of Society*, translated by Kathleen Blamey. Cambridge, MA: MIT Press, 1998.

Castoriadis, Cornelius. 'Intervention de Cornelius Castoriadis.' In *De la fin de l'histoire*, edited by Jean-Luc Boilleau. Paris: Éditions du Félin, 1992.

Castoriadis, Cornelius. 'Modern Capitalism and Revolution.' In *Political and Social Writings, Volume 2: 1955–1960*, edited and translated by David A. Curtis, 226–344. Minneapolis: University of Minnesota Press, 1988.

Castoriadis, Cornelius. 'La Montée de l'insignifiance.' In *La Montée de l'insignifiance, Les Carrefours du labyrinth IV*, 82–102. Paris: Éditions du Seuil, 1996.

Castoriadis, Cornelius. *La Montée de l'insignifiance, Les Carrefours du labyrinth IV*. Paris: Éditions du Seuil, 1996.

Castoriadis, Cornelius. 'No God, No Caesar, No Tribune!,' translated by Gabriel Rockhill and the Villanova Translation Workshop. In *Postscript on Insignificance: Dialogues with Cornelius Castoriadis*, trans. Gabriel Rockhill and John V. Garner, 5–19. New York: Continuum, 2011.

Castoriadis, Cornelius. *On Plato's Statesman*, translated by David A. Curtis. Stanford: Stanford University Press, 1999.

Castoriadis, Cornelius. 'On the Content of Socialism, I–III.' In *Political and Social Writings, Volume 1: 1946–1955*, edited and translated by David A. Curtis, 290–333. Minneapolis: University of Minnesota Press, 1988; and *Political and Social Writings, Volume 2: 1955–1960*, edited and translated by David A. Curtis, 90–192. Minneapolis: University of Minnesota Press, 1988.

Castoriadis, Cornelius. *Philosophy, Politics, Autonomy: Essays in Political Philosophy*, edited and translated by David. A. Curtis. New York: Oxford University Press, 1991.

Castoriadis, Cornelius. *Political and Social Writings, Volume 1: 1946–1955*, edited and translated by David A. Curtis. Minneapolis: University of Minnesota Press, 1988.

Castoriadis, Cornelius. *Political and Social Writings, Volume 2: 1955–1960*, edited and translated by David A. Curtis. Minneapolis: University of Minnesota Press, 1988.

Castoriadis, Cornelius. *Political and Social Writings, Volume 3: 1961–1979*, edited and translated by David A. Curtis. Minneapolis: University of Minnesota Press, 1988.

Castoriadis, Cornelius. *Postscript on Insignificance: Dialogues with Cornelius Castoriadis*, edited by Gabriel Rockhill and translated by Gabriel Rockhill and John V. Garner. New York: Continuum, 2011.

Castoriadis, Cornelius. 'Power, Politics, Autonomy.' In *Philosophy, Politics, Autonomy: Essays in Political Philosophy*, edited and translated by David. A. Curtis, 143–74. New York: Oxford University Press, 1991.

Castoriadis, Cornelius. 'Reflections on Racism.' In *World in Fragments: Writings on Politics, Society, Psychoanalysis, and the Imagination*, edited and translated by David A. Curtis, 19–31. Stanford: Stanford University Press, 1997.

Castoriadis, Cornelius. 'Reflections on "Rationality" and "Development".' In *Philosophy, Politics, Autonomy: Essays in Political Philosophy*, edited and translated by David. A. Curtis, 175–218. New York: Oxford University Press, 1991.

Castoriadis, Cornelius. 'The Retreat from Autonomy: Postmodernism as Generalized Conformism.' In *World in Fragments: Writings on Politics, Society, Psychoanalysis, and the Imagination*, edited and translated by David A. Curtis, 32–43. Stanford: Stanford University Press, 1997.

Castoriadis, Cornelius. *Sujet et vérité dans le monde social-historique, Séminaires 1986–1987. La création humaine I*. Paris: Éditions du Seuil, 2002.

Castoriadis, Cornelius. *Thucydide, la force et le droit, Ce qui fait la Grèce, tome 3. Séminaires 1984–1985*. Paris: Éditions du Seuil, 2011.

REFERENCES

Castoriadis, Cornelius. 'Time and Creation.' In *World in Fragments: Writings on Politics, Society, Psychoanalysis, and the Imagination*, edited and translated by David A. Curtis, 374–401. Stanford: Stanford University Press, 1997.

Castoriadis, Cornelius. *World in Fragments: Writings on Politics, Society, Psychoanalysis, and the Imagination*, edited and translated by David A. Curtis. Stanford: Stanford University Press, 1997.

Clastres, Pierre. *Chronicle of the Guayaki Indians*, translated by Paul Auster. New York: Zone Books, 2000.

Clastres, Pierre. *Recherches d'anthropologie politique*. Paris: Éditions du Seuil, 1980.

Clastres, Pierre. *Society Against the State: Essays in Political Anthropology*, translated by Robert Hurley and Abe Stein. New York: Zone Books, 1989.

Clastres, Pierre. 'Of Torture in Primitive Societies.' In *Society Against the State: Essays in Political Anthropology*, translated by Robert Hurley and Abe Stein, 177–88. New York: Zone Books, 1989.

Constant, Benjamin. 'The Liberty of the Ancients Compared with that of the Moderns.' In *Political Writings*, edited and translated by Biancamaria Fontana, 309–28. Cambridge: Cambridge University Press, 1988.

Constant, Benjamin. *Political Writings*, edited and translated by Biancamaria Fontana. Cambridge: Cambridge University Press, 1988.

Descartes, René. *Discourse on Method: Third Edition*, translated by Donald A. Cress. Indianapolis: Hackett, 1998.

Dewitte, Jacques. 'Indétermination et contraction, ou de l'anneau de Gygès à l'Alliance.' *Cahiers d'études Levinasiennes*, no. 2 (2003): 101–29.

Diderot, Denis. *Jacques the Fatalist*, translated by David Coward. Oxford: Oxford World Classics, 2009.

Dosse, François. *Castoriadis : Une vie*. Paris: La Découverte, 2014.

Dzimira, Sylvain. 'Antiutilitarisme et décroissance. Compte-rendu.' *La Revue du MAUSS permanente*, 11 August 2007. http://www.journaldumauss.net/./?Antiutilitarisme-et-decroissance.

Eco, Umberto. 'Ur-Fascism.' *The New York Review of Books*, 22 June 1995.

Ferguson, Adam. *An Essay on the History of Civil Society*. Cambridge: Cambridge University Press, 1996.

Ferry, Luc and Alain Renaut. *68–86 Itinéraires de l'individu*. Paris: Gallimard, 1987.

Ferry, Luc and Alain Renaut. *French Philosophy of the Sixties: An Essay on Antihumanism*, translated by Mary H.S. Cattani. Amherst: The University of Massachusetts Press, 1990.

Fukuyama, Francis. 'The End of History?' *The National Interest*, no. 16 (Summer 1989): 3–18.

Fukuyama, Francis. *The End of History and the Last Man*. New York: Free Press, 1992.

Fukuyama, Francis. 'La fin de l'histoire ?' *Commentaire* 47, no. 3 (1989): 457–69.

Gadamer, Hans-Georg. *Dialogue and Dialectic: Eight Hermeneutical Studies of Plato*, translated by P. Christopher Smith. New Haven: Yale University Press, 1980.

Gadamer, Hans-Georg. 'Plato's Unwritten Dialectic.' In *Dialogue and Dialectic: Eight Hermeneutical Studies of Plato*, translated by P. Christopher Smith, 124–55. New Haven: Yale University Press, 1980.

Garner, John V. 'Cornelius Castoriadis.' *Internet Encyclopedia of Philosophy* (2011/2015). https://www.iep.utm.edu/castoria/.

Garner, John V. *The Emerging Good in Plato's Philebus*. Evanston: Northwestern University Press, 2017.

Girard, René. *Violence and the Sacred*, translated by Patrick Gregory. Baltimore: Johns Hopkins University Press, 1977.

Gourgouris, Stathis. 'Philosophy and Sublimation.' *Thesis Eleven* 49, no. 1 (1997): 31–43.

Graeber, David. 'Give it Away.' In *These Times* 24, no. 19 (2000), retrieved 29 May 2019. https://inthesetimes.com/issue/24/19/graeber2419.html

Hansen, Mogens H. *The Athenian Democracy in the Age of Demosthenes: Structure, Principles, and Ideology*, translated by J.A. Crook. Norman: University of Oklahoma Press, 1999.

Hansen, Mogens H. *Polis: An Introduction to the Ancient Greek City-State*, translated by J.A. Crook. Oxford: Oxford University Press, 2006.

Hayek, Friedrich August von. *The Road to Serfdom*. London: Routledge Press, 1944.

Klimis, Sophie. 'La Pensée au travail. Réinventer l'autonomie à partir de Platon.' In *Cornelius Castoriadis. Réinventer l'autonomie*, edited by Blaise Bachofen, Sion Elbaz, and Nicolas Poirier, 235–49. Paris: Éditions du Sandre, 2008.

Klooger, Jeff. 'Anlehnung (Leaning On).' In *Cornelius Castoriadis: Key Concepts*, edited by Suzi Adams, 127–34. London: Bloomsbury, 2014.

Klooger, Jeff. *Castoriadis: Psyche, Society, Autonomy*. Boston: Brill, 2009.

Klooger, Jeff. 'Ensemblist-Identitary Logic (Ensidic Logic).' In *Cornelius Castoriadis: Key Concepts*, edited by Suzi Adams, 108–16. London: Bloomsbury, 2014.

Kolakowski, Leszek. *L'Esprit révolutionnaire*. Brussels: Complexe, 1978.

Lao-tzu. *Tao Te Ching*, translated by Steven Addis and Stanley Lombardo. Indianapolis: Hackett, 1993.

Latouche, Serge. *The Westernization of the World: Significance, Scope and Limits of the Drive Towards Global Uniformity*. Cambridge: Polity Press, 1996.

Lefort, Claude. *Democracy and Political Theory*, translated by David Macey. Cambridge: Polity Press, 1988.

Lefort, Claude. 'Réflexions sur le projet du MAUSS.' *La Revue du MAUSS semestrielle*, no. 2 (1993): 61–79.

Leibniz, G.W. 'Dialogue (1677).' In *Philosophical Essays*, translated by Roger Ariew and Daniel Garber, 268–72. Indianapolis: Hackett, 1989.

Leibniz, G.W. *Philosophical Essays*, translated by Roger Ariew and Daniel Garber. Indianapolis: Hackett, 1989.

Lévi-Strauss, Claude. *Race and History*. Paris: UNESCO, 1952.

Lévi-Strauss, Claude. *Structural Anthropology, Volume 2*, translated by Monique Layton. Chicago: University of Chicago Press, 1983.

Luhmann, Niklas. *Politique et complexité. Les contributions de la théorie générale des systems*. Paris: Éditions du Cerf, 1999.

REFERENCES

Marx, Karl and Fredric Engels. *The Marx-Engels Reader: Second Edition*, edited by Robert Tucker. New York: W.W. Norton and Co., 1978.

Marx, Karl. *The Poverty of Philosophy*. Beijing: Foreign Language Press, 1978.

Mauss, Marcel. *The Gift: The Form and Reason for Exchange in Archaic Societies*, translated by W.D. Halls. Abingdon: Routledge, 1990.

Michéa, Jean-Claude. 'Introduction de Jean-Claude Michéa.' In *De la fin de l'histoire*, edited by Jean-Luc Boilleau. Paris: Éditions du Félin, 1992.

Montaigne, Michel de. *Essays*, translated by J.M. Cohen. London: Penguin, 1993.

Mouzakitis, Angelos. 'Creation *ex nihilo*.' In *Cornelius Castoriadis: Key Concepts*, edited by Suzi Adams, 53–64. London: Bloomsbury, 2014.

Nodier, Luc Marie (pseudonym of Jean-Louis Cherlonneix). *Anatomie du Bien : Explication et commentaire des principales idées de Platon concernant le plaisir et la souffrance, la bonne façon de vivre, et la vie en generale*. Paris: La Découverte, 1996.

Paulhan, Jean. 'Preface.' In Pauline Réage, *Story of O*, translated by Sabine D'Estrée, xxi–xxxvi. New York: Grove Press, 1965.

Plato. *Complete Works*, edited by John M. Cooper. Indianapolis: Hackett, 1997.

Prat, Jean-Louis. 'Anatomie d'un mirage.' *La Revue du MAUSS semestrielle*, no. 8 (1996): 360–66.

Prat, Jean-Louis, *Introduction à Castoriadis*. Paris: La Découverte, 2007.

Réage, Pauline. *Story of O*, translated by Sabine D'Estrée. New York: Grove Press, 1965.

Robespierre, Maximilien. *Oeuvres complètes de Maximilien Robespierre, 10 volumes*. Paris: Société des études Robespierristes, 1950–1967.

Rockhill, Gabriel. *Counter-History of the Present: Untimely Interrogations into Globalization, Technology, Democracy*. Durham: Duke University Press, 2017.

Rockhill, Gabriel. 'Editor's Introduction: Eros of Inquiry: An *Aperçu* of Castoriadis' Life and Work.' In *Postscript on Insignificance: Dialogues with Cornelius Castoriadis*, translated by Gabriel Rockhill and John V. Garner, ix–xxxix. New York: Continuum, 2011.

Rockhill, Gabriel. 'What is the Use of Democracy?: Urgency of an Inappropriate Question,' translated by John V. Garner. In *Counter-History of the Present: Untimely Interrogations into Globalization, Technology, Democracy*, 51–102. Durham: Duke University Press, 2017.

Rousseau, Jean-Jacques. *The Social Contract and Other Later Political Writings*, translated by Victor Gourevich. Cambridge: Cambridge University Press, 1997.

Sade, Marquis de. *The 120 Days of Sodom*, translated by Will McMorran and Thomas Wynn. London: Penguin Books, 2016.

Sartre, Jean-Paul. *Search for a Method*, trans. Hazel E. Barnes. New York: Alfred A. Knopf, 1963.

Sidane, Victor, ed. *Le Printemps de Pékin, Oppositions démocratique en Chine, novembre 1978–mars 1980*. Paris: Gallimard/Julliard, 1980.

Smith, Karl E. 'Modernity.' in *Cornelius Castoriadis: Key Concepts*, edited by Suzi Adams, 179–90. London: Bloomsbury, 2014.

'Soudan, persécutions contre des chrétiens dans le sud du pays.' *Le Monde*. 9 December 1994.

Straume, Ingerid S. 'Castoriadis, Education and Democracy.' In *Creation, Rationality, and Autonomy: Essays on Cornelius Castoriadis*, edited by Ingerid S. Straume and Giorgio Baruchello, 203–28. Copenhagen: NSU Press, 2013.

Straume, Ingerid S. and Giorgio Baruchello, eds. *Creation, Rationality, and Autonomy: Essays on Cornelius Castoriadis*. Copenhagen: NSU Press, 2013.

Straume, Ingerid S. 'Paideia.' In *Cornelius Castoriadis: Key Concepts*, edited by Suzi Adams, 143–53. London: Bloomsbury, 2014.

Testart, Jacques. 'Jacques Testart, critique de science,' accessed 25 May 2019 http://jacques.testart.free.fr/.

Tocqueville, Alexis de. *The Ancien Régime and the French Revolution*, translated by Arthur Goldhammer. Cambridge: Cambridge University Press, 2011.

Vakaloulis, Michel and Jean-Marie Vincent, eds. *Marx après les marxismes, tome 1*. Paris: L'Harmattan, 1997.

Vernant, Jean-Pierre. *Myth and Thought among the Greeks*, translated by Janet Lloyd and Jeff Fort. New York: Zone Books, 2006.

INDEX

agora, xix, 12, 39, 89n29
ancestors, appeals to, xii, xvii, xxixn36, 15
'anonymous collective', xxivn13, 88n22
Aquinas, Thomas, 46
arrangement (*disposition*), 60, 65, 70–72, 77, 93n55
Aristotle, xxviin28, 46, 62, 72, 83
autonomy, viii–x, xiv–xvi, 55, 64; 'autonomous society', 5, 58, 65–66, 80; Castoriadis on, 15, 26, 34, 36, 40, 49, 60, 63, 64–65, 80; Dewitte on, 6; effective, xvi, xxixn33; intercultural versions of, xxvn21; privilege of, xxviin29

Bacon, Francis, 38, 40, 89n28
Badinter, Élisabeth, 83
Baechler, Jean, 11, 48, 52, 53, 55, 56, 91n46
Balladur, Édouard, 24, 60, 80, 85n6
barbarism, 13
Barel, Yves, 60
Baslé, Louis, xviii
Bastille Day celebrations, 43
Bataille, Georges, 2
Baudelaire, Charles, 41
Benedict, Ruth, 54

Berbers, 52, 53
Berlusconi, Silvio, 60
Bernal, Martin, xxviiin31
Berthoud, Gérard, 1
Boas, Franz, 2
Boilleau, Jean-Luc, 2, 5, 7
Bourdieu, Pierre, 1
Bouygues S.A., 60
Buddhism, 31, 40
Bush, George H. W., 79

Caillé, Alain, vii, viii, xiv, xviii, 1, 6, 66, 70, 72, 74, 80, 82; letter for *MAUSS* debate, 23–24, 26, 27, 52; on *MAUSS* and Marxism, 3–4, 4, 11
capitalism, xi, 2, 4, 8–9, 9, 40, 46, 49, 78
Castoriadis, Cornelius: on autonomy, 15, 26, 34, 36, 40, 49, 60, 63, 64–66, 80; background of, vii, x, xviii–xix, 1, 64; on Christianity, 46–48; on collapse of Western society, 25, 29, 36, 42–43; on Europe, 15, 26; on Greek culture, 26–27, 28, 29, 33, 40, 41, 46, 49, 53, 70–72, 83; Marxism and, 2, 3–4, 4, 10, 11, 27, 41, 46, 49, 60, 64; on *MAUSS*, 23–24; resources on, xxi; on the

United States, 29, 69, 70, 73, 75, 78
Castoriadis, Cornelius, publications by: 'Dead End?', 83; 'Democracy as Procedure and Democracy as Regime', 60; *Devant la guerre*, 17n14; 'Done and To Be Done', 58, 70, 80–81; *The Imaginary Institution of Society*, xix, 9; 'On the Content of Socialism', 60; 'Reflections on "Rationality" and "Development"', 81–82
Cherlonneix, Jean-Louis, 2
China, 28, 33, 37, 39, 49; dissidents in, 15, 22n48, 36
Chirac, Jacques, 60, 80, 93n57, 96n75
Clastres, Pierre, 3, 4, 6, 11, 28, 54, 58, 87n14
climate change, 81
colonialism, 13, 53
Confucius, 28
Constant, Benjamin, 62, 67, 78
creation, 12, 32, 87n21
cultural norms, viii

Darwinism, 53
democracy, 52–82; in ancient Greece, viii, xiv–xvi, xxviiin31, xxixn33, 9, 12, 49, 52, 52–53, 54, 62, 70–72, 92n49; Baechler on, 53, 91n46; Baslé on, 49; in China, 35; 'consensual', 57; creation and, xi, 39; direct, 6, 55, 58–62, 67–69, 74, 76, 77; fragility of, ix, 55; indeterminacy and, 12, 25, 32; Lefort on, x, xxiiin11, 24, 85n7; Marx on, 9; oligarchies and, xv, xxviiin28; participation in, xi–xii, xix, xxivn14; as 'regime', 49, 52, 55, 58–60, 69; superiority of, 15, 80
Descartes, René, 40, 89n27
determinacy, xi, xv, 4, 8, 20n30, 32
Dewitte, Jacques, xviii, 6, 66
dialogue, xiv, xxvin22
Diderot, Denis, 1
doxai, 76

economic imaginary, 80–81, 82. *See also* market economy
education, viii, xi, xxivn14, 58, 77
ekklēsia, xix, 60, 89n29
'end of history' thesis, 6–8
ensemblist-identitary works, 9, 20n30
ethnocentrism, xiv, xvi, xxiin4, xxviin29, 13, 26
Eurocentricism, 11, 27
exploitation, 10, 20n36, 40, 41

Fehér, Ferenc, 81
Ferguson, Adam, 62
Ferry, Luc, and Alain Renault, 6
feudalism, 9, 49, 57
Fixot, Anne-Marie, xviii
Freud, Sigmund, 64
Fukuyama, Francis, 6–8, 19n26

Gaddafi, Muammar, 29
germ metaphor, xv, 27, 35, 44, 62, 86n9
gift, the, 1, 2, 24, 82, 84n2
Girard, René, xxvn17
Gorbachev, Mikhail, 6
Graber, David, 84n2
Greece, ancient, 13, 44, 49; democracy in, viii, xiv–xvi, xxviiin31, xxixn33, 9, 49, 54, 62, 70–72; faults in, xxviin25, 29, 41. *See also* Castoriadis, Cornelius: on Greek culture

Habermas, Jürgen, 60
Hayek, Friedrich, 53
Hegel, Georg Wilhelm Friedrich, 8, 33
Heidegger, Martin, xv, 40, 46
Herodotus, 13, 27
heteronomy, xii, xiii, xv, xvi, xxivn12, xxviin29, 16, 53, 56, 58, 60, 65; primitive societies and, 21n40, 49; sortition and, xxixn36
Hitler, Adolf, 70
Homer, 46
homosexuality, 75

INDEX

hope, xxvn20, 3, 43
humanism, 44–46

indeterminacy, xi, 12, 31–32, 48, 49, 54, 60, 85n7
India, 33, 36, 37, 87n16
individualism, xii, xxvn16; pseudo-individualism, xii, xix; interlocutory individuals and, xiii
instrumentalization (of nature and humans), 40, 41, 46
Islam, 15, 29, 36

Judaism, 48, 65

kleroterion machines, xvi
Kohl, Helmut, 60
Kojève, Alexandre, 2
Kolakowski, Leszek, 6, 17n14

Laguiller, Arlette, 80, 96n75
Las Casas, Bartolomé de, 27, 48
Latouche, Serge, viii, xviii, 4, 6, 23, 66, 82
Lefort, Claude, x, 6, 12, 23, 24, 48, 54, 55, 56, 57, 60; Caillé's defense of, 24, 85n4
Leibniz, Gottfried Wilhelm, 40
Levinas, Emmanuel, 6
Lévi-Strauss, Claude, 13
Louis XV, 69
Luhmann, Niklas, 75

magistrates, 60, 66, 93n58
market economy, 24, 49, 53, 78, 84n2
Marx, Karl (and Marxism), xvii, xviii, 2–4, 8–9, 9–10, 11, 18n16, 27, 41, 49, 62, 64
MAUSS (Mouvement Anti-Utilitariste en Sciences Sociales): background of, 1–2; Castoriadis on, 24; markets and, 24; Marxism and, 2–4
Mauss, Marcel, 1–2, 3, 84n2
Michéa, Jean-Claude, 7–9
Mill, John Stuart, 68

Mitchell, Margaret, 35
modernity, 7, 24, 89n30
Montaigne, Michel de, 13, 27
Montesquieu, Charles-Louis de Secondat, 27
Morin, Edgar, 7
Mouffe, Chantal, xviii, 6, 68

Napoleon Bonaparte, 75
nature, 38, 40–41, 46
nihilism, xiii

oikos, xix
Orwell, George 85n8

paideia, xi, 60, 77, 92n53
Paul, Saint, 48
Paulhan, Jean, 76
phronēsis, 83, 97n83
Plato, xxvin22, 30, 32, 46, 75, 76, 77, 95n73
pluralism, 68, 74, 75, 82
Plutarch, 13
Polanyi, Karl, 3, 4, 18n16
political positions, right to, 12, 33–34
politics (*la politique*) vs. the political (*le politique*), xi, 27–28, 86n12
Popper, Karl, 12
'post-truth era,', viii
power, three functions of, 54
Prat, Jean-Louis, xviii
'primary sociality', xiii, 42, 90n33
privatization, xi, 48, 49, 91n45
Proust, Marcel, 57

'radical imagination', xxiiin6, 12, 30, 33, 49, 88n22
'radical instituting imaginary', 12–13, 30, 33, 49, 88n22
rationality, 40
'rational mastery', 40, 41, 44, 46, 89n30
relativism: challenges of, ix–x; consequences of, viii; cultural, 13, 26, 28–29, 30–31, 33–35, 85n8
Robespierre, Maximilien, 36

Roman Empire, 13, 34, 46
Rousseau, Jean-Jacques, 8, 13, 49, 60, 68, 69, 72

Sade, Marquis de, 75
Saint-Simon, Henri de, 8, 9
Sartre, Jean-Paul, 2
scholarship, xiii, xvii
'secondary sociality', 90n33
self-questioning, xiv, 30, 31, 39, 42, 55, 56, 75
self-institution, xiii, 54, 55–56, 60, 64
Socialisme ou Barbarie, x, 17n14, 60
slavery, 31, 35, 38, 41, 44–46, 72; in ancient Greece, xxviin25, 29, 41, 46; Christianity and, 46
Socrates, 75
solidarity, 42, 44

sortition, xvi, xxixn36, 12
Stalin, Joseph, 12, 83
Stoicism, 46, 48
Swift, Jonathan, 27

Taoism, 31, 35, 40
Tao Te Ching, 28
technology, limits of, 83
Testart, Jacques, 83
theory (*theōrein*), 33
Thucydides, 46
Tocqueville, Alexis de, 42, 49, 49–52
totalitarianism, x, 3, 5, 17n14, 37, 39

United States, 29, 69, 70, 72, 75, 78–80
universalism, 5, 13, 13–15, 30, 35, 36, 40, 46

Vernant, Jean-Pierre, 12

www.ingramcontent.com/pod-product-compliance
Lightning Source LLC
Chambersburg PA
CBHW030122240426
43673CB00041B/1368